Vicki Lansky's

# BIRTHDAY PARTIES

Book Trade Distribution
Publisher's Group West
Emeryville, California

**the book peddlers**
deephaven, mn

Special editorial thanks to: Kathryn Ring   Sandra Whelan
                             Theresa Early   Julie Surma
                             Toni Burbank

Also:  Deephaven Montessori School
       Nancy Wiederhold
       Linda Moorhead
       Mary McNamara
       Linda Wiegel

Illustrator:  Jack Lindstrom
Cover Design and Art Direction: MacLean & Tuminelly

Special thanks to the parents who shared their words and
feelings. Their quotes are reprinted with permission from
Vicki Lansky's *Practical Parenting* newsletter.

BIRTHDAY PARTIES

*A Bantam Book / August 1986*
*revised and updated edition*
*The Book Peddlers / May 1989*

ISBN 0-916773-10-8

For group sales or quantity discounts contact:
The Book Peddlers
18326 Minnetonka Blvd.
Deephaven, MN 55391
(612) 475-3527

10 9 8 7

# Contents

## Introduction
# Who, Me, Give a Party?

Yes, you can give a wonderful birthday party for your young child that is as much fun for you as for the birthday child and the guests. These younger years are a very special time. By the time kids are in elementary school, they have very definite ideas about their own parties—which might not coincide with yours. This is a chance to focus on your child and create memories that will last a lifetime. Besides, birthday parties are a tremendous boost to any child's self-esteem. A happy day of one's own is the best birthday gift you can give your child.

The basic components of any party are really quite simple: invitations, decorations, presents, cake and ice cream, favors, and some planned activities. Don't try to include every idea you've ever heard or read about (that includes the ideas in this book, too!) or you'll be exhausted and the kids will be overwhelmed. Give the kind of party you enjoy giving—not the one you think you "should" give. Too often, parents look upon a birthday party as a ritual to be endured, or as an opportunity to make a lavish party for their own friends.

For young children, these are the best rules to follow:

- *KEEP IT SMALL.*
- *KEEP IT SHORT.*
- *KEEP IT SIMPLE.*
- *KEEP IT MOVING.*
- *AND KEEP YOUR SENSE OF HUMOR!*

# Where Do I Start? Getting Organized

Successful birthday parties don't happen by magic; the good ones are planned. It's important to bear in mind that any child's birthday party, after the first one, is for him or her, not for you. Forget showing off either your child or your decorating talents. A party must be fun for your child and the guests. Keeping it manageable, yet flexible, is the secret of success. And planning is the key!

You can plan in your head, but most of us need to put our plans and ideas down on paper. Provided here and throughout the book are checklists you can photocopy and use as you plan your party. Or they may simply provide you with some thoughts as you make your own lists.

You are going to need to consider:

—Invitations
—Decorations
—Favors
—Prizes, if any
—Cake
—Ice cream

—Other food
—Paper supplies
—Camera and film
—Party area/location
—Activities
—Supplies for activities

# Budget Considerations

Even the simplest birthday parties cost money. What you should spend is only what you can afford to spend. Obviously, the more you create from scratch, the less the party will cost.

- A good way to save money is not to serve a meal. Cake and ice cream are the main components of any party, and if you provide those, you will really have done it all.

- Activities away from home that carry a high price tag can be offset by limiting the number of guests.

- Spending to compete with your neighbors will be something only you are aware of—your child won't, at least not for several more years.

# Age Considerations

Considering what your child is ready for at his or her specific age will go a long way to helping you plan a successful day. Children grow and change dramatically from year to year, so you need to rethink your approach for each birthday.

### Age 1

Ones have absolutely no concept of parties, despite the significance of the occasion. Schedules and formal games are unnecessary. But since the first birthday is such a landmark, it has a section all its own in Chapter 4. Keep the party short: ½ to 1 hour will more than suffice.

### Age 2

Twos are demanding, possessive, and grabby and can't truly grasp the idea of a party. Parties need to be planned with their social immaturity in mind, and with their parent(s) included. A party with a few favorite adults can be just as satisfying for a

2-year-old as one with two or three other children. Supervised parallel play and a few activities will occupy a child of 2 and a few friends. Remember that small children have small attention spans. No 2-year-old remembers a first birthday party, so whatever you do will be new and exciting. A party for this age need only be 1 to 1½ hours long.

## Age 3

Children of 3 and up usually love a party. Those who are used to group situations can usually handle a party very well. If your child is shy or a loner, keep that in mind when setting up your party plan. Keep the party fairly informal. Avoid loud, rough games because they may overstimulate children at this age. Separate quarreling children; it is better to remove a difficult child than to punish the child—after all, this is a party. Children of 3 will enjoy both group games and solitary play. In fact, too many group games can overwhelm them and some may *need* to sit alone and play with an assortment of unbreakable toys from the birthday child's collection. Guests of this age have been known to want to take their own gifts home with them, so don't be surprised if you have to deal with behavior problems. Between 1 and 2 hours should be enough time.

## Age 4

Children of 4 understand the idea of a birthday party just for them and really appreciate it and get excited about it. Discipline is usually not a problem at this age. Still, speed and simplicity are in order. You will need short games, and you must keep the party moving because 4-year-olds find it hard to wait their turn. Hunts of all kinds are appreciated from this age and up. A good story, simple arts and crafts projects, and games will all be enjoyed. Physical energy abounds, so plan to channel it. Party time of 1½ hours, but not more than 2½ hours, will work well.

## Age 5

Children of 5 feel that parties are important and sometimes enjoy the planning and the anticipation even more than the party itself. While children of this age may seem self-contained and capable, the highly charged atmosphere of a party can be hard for a 5-year-old to handle. Theme party ideas work well with this age. It is still hard for children of 5 to take turns, and they will need to be entertained steadily. Same-sex parties start to emerge for some at this age. Be sure to mark guests' take-home items clearly, because 5-year-olds don't like to "lose" things or get their possessions mixed up with others'. Parties away from home can work, but you still run the risk of overwhelming your child and/or the guests. Be conservative in the place you pick and the number of guests you invite if you'll be outside the house. The ideal length of parties for this age is about 2 hours.

Elementary-age children love parties, love the traditions, and eagerly plan and participate in all of it. A sense of fairness will be evident; theme parties are enjoyed; fewer children are fussy eaters. Parties away from home can work well from this age and on. Children often begin by this time to have their own ideas of how they want their party to be run. Do listen to them. After all, it's their day! Parties of 2 to 2½ hours are fine. Parties for any age should not exceed 3 hours, or the children will get tired, overexcited, and hard to handle.

## Choosing the Date

Plan the party for a day that's convenient for you, one when you'll have adequate help. Weekends are better, for example, if you want help from your spouse or a school-age sitter.

- Try to set the party date for the actual birthday, but don't be rigid about it. Kids don't care that much. However, if the party isn't on the child's birthday, you will probably find yourself celebrating twice!

- If your child's birthday falls on a holiday, remember that potential guests may have other plans. Send out invitations extra early, or consider having the party another day.

- Take school schedules into account. If some of the children are in kindergarten, both morning and afternoon may be out, and both kindergarten and nursery school children may be too tired to enjoy a party on a school day. If the birthday is on a school day and you decide to save the celebration for the weekend, you can still make the birthday special by having your child take some treats to school to share with friends.

- Don't hesitate to call parents to check on the schedules of best friends without whom the party won't be a success.

> My husband, a dentist, confessed that he believed for some years that all our children had been born on Wednesday—until he realized that Wednesday happened to be his day off.
>
> *Betty James, New London, CT*

## Choosing the Hours

- Consider morning, afternoon, and early evening hours. Aim for the time that best suits your child's schedule, and keep in mind that some children take naps, even if yours doesn't. Late morning on a Saturday may be your best choice if you have to work around naps and schedules. If you're past nap-taking age, and if you're not serving a meal, 1 to 3 PM can be ideal—after lunch and early enough so dinner won't be spoiled.

- Don't try to make a marathon of the party and a martyr of yourself. Exceptions to the brief party rule may be extra time for a party held at a picnic ground, skating rink, or some other away-from-home place, and an extra half-hour for a party at which a full meal is served.

- *Do* plan the end of the party as well as the beginning. If you're worried that some parents may not pick up their children on time, plan to take them home yourself so the party will end on *your* time schedule.

> Evening parties seem to be the worst. Kids are too tired.
>
> *Dana Wynne, Louisville, KY*

# Making up the Guest List

Although parties and crowds may go hand in hand for adults, this is *not* the case for little children. A large party, even if all the children know each other, can be overwhelming for you as well as for the kids. If you really want to include every member of your child's preschool class, send the treats and favors to school—don't invite everyone to your home. For those not invited (neighbors, cousins, uncles), save a piece of cake and a balloon to share with them later.

If the children are 1 or 2 years old, you'll want to have at least 1 parent present for each child; after 3, children usually behave better and have more fun if their own parents aren't present. When other parents *are* present at your party, despite your best intentions, you will find yourself catering to their needs as well as those of the children. Ultimately, this is very exhausting and seldom satisfying.

Remember that the more similar the ages of the guests, the more likely it is that the party will go smoothly.

- Let your child help with the guest list. You should offer choices or make suggestions, don't just ask an open-ended question about who the child wants to invite. Sometimes there is a guest you know must be invited and you will have to be firm about such a decision, but give weight to your child's feelings about this rather than dismissing them lightly.

- Invite 1 guest for each year of your child's life, say some, or 1 for each year, plus 1 (5 children for a fourth birthday, for example).

- Or follow one professional party entertainer's rule: If you're courageous, if the birthday child is at least 4 years old, and if you have good help, 8 to 15 children may be ideal for the most fun.

- Parties for boys will need to move faster than those for

girls. Generally speaking, boys' energy levels are higher and their attention spans shorter.

- Plan on including siblings unless they're liable to be *very* disruptive. An older child may be able to help with games and serving, and you may invite Grandma or get a sitter to help with a very young child. It's important to be sure the birthday child will not be upstaged, though.

## Hired—or Acquired—Help

Everything will be much easier if you have help—a spouse, friend, relative, older sibling, or babysitter who will assist with games and activities as well as with serving and cleanup.

Helpers can make the difference between a frantic versus a smooth-running party. While you cut the cake, your helper can be pouring drinks; while you monitor one game, your helper can be setting up for the next one. At first and second birthday parties, you'll probably have at least one parent for each child available for extra help, but after that you're on your own.

Helpers can also be in charge of taking pictures, grilling hamburgers, providing face-painting, and helping children find the bathroom.

The best ratio is generally 2 adults to 8 children; but 2 adults are the minimum required to keep things running smoothly in most cases. Here are some ideas for finding and working with party helpers:

- Spouses can be important helpmates in running a party smoothly. Discuss beforehand in detail how to share the party chores and entertainment.

- A good friend who is the parent of one of the party guests can be recruited and the favor can later be reciprocated.

- Grandparents can be "organized" to assist, but only if that is their style. If they don't visit regularly or help out in your home, this is not the time to recruit them.

- Teens aged 14 to 16 make excellent helpers. They join in games more enthusiastically and less condescendingly than adults.

- Hire your child's regular babysitter and be specific in what you will need help with. Don't pay by regular hourly sitters' rates. Pay a flat fee that makes this worthwhile to both of you.

- Hire an older sibling or step-sibling and make this a real job with a solid fee. Make sure he or she understands that cleanup is included.

- Assign specific jobs to *someone*, whether yourself or your helper(s), so there is no confusion about who will be scooping ice cream or getting out the next activity.

## Father Involvement

- Encourage (and a lot of encouragement may be needed) Dad to help with every detail of party planning, from the guest list to the choice of games to the departure hour.

- Put Dad in charge of any decorations that can be set up the night before the party, such as hanging mobiles and streamers (no crepe paper streamers outdoors before the day of the party, though), clearing out and arranging the party room, setting the table.

- Consider scheduling the party for a time when he may be able to participate fully or at least arrive home in time to drive the guests home and/or help with the cleanup.

# PRELIMINARY PLANNING LIST

Birthday Child's Age:_____ Date:_____ Day of Week _____
Time:_____ Place: _____
Theme (if using one): _____
Entertainer (if using one): _____
Number of Guests:_____ Number of Invitations Needed: _____
Helpers on Hand: _____

_____

## Guest List

Children:

| Full Name | Address | Phone # | Name of Parent | Reply |
|-----------|---------|---------|----------------|-------|
| | | | | |
| | | | | |
| | | | | |
| | | | | |
| | | | | |
| | | | | |
| | | | | |

Adult Friends and Relatives:

| Name | Address | Phone # | Reply |
|------|---------|---------|-------|
| | | | |
| | | | |
| | | | |

## Away-from-Home Party Possibilities [repeat as needed for each place]

Place/Address _____
Phone_____Fee _____
Services Included _____

_____
Menu _____
Special Considerations _____

# SHOPPING LIST

**Paper Products and Such:**
Invitations: _____
Stamps: _____
Plates: _____
Cups: _____
Tablecloth: _____
Place Mats: _____
Candles: _____
Forks and Spoons: _____
Balloons: _____
Decorations: _____
_____
_____
Favors: _____
_____
Arts and Crafts Supplies: _____
_____
Prizes: _____
_____

**Food:**
Cake: _____
  Order From: _____
  _____
  Phone: _____
  Order Date: _____
  Pickup Date & Time _____
  _____
  Homemade (Ingredients): _____
  _____
  _____
  Frosting: _____
Ice Cream: _____
Food Favors: _____
_____
Drink: _____
Food for a Meal: _____
_____
_____
For a Treasure Hunt: _____
_____

Materials for Activities and Crafts (from Activity Planner List):
_____
_____
_____
_____
_____

## And Don't Forget:
Camara (or VCR): _____
Film: _____
Casette Recorder: _____

Tapes: _____
Trash Bags for Cleanup: _____

# What Kind of Party Will It Be?

For small children home parties work best. They find it exciting to have a party with friends in familiar and comfortable surroundings. You don't have to have an elaborate party for it to be enjoyable. As you begin to plan, you will need to think about the ages of your guests, the space you have available, and the time of year.

Before you send out invitations you'll need to decide whether the party will be indoors or outdoors so your guests will know what clothing will be appropriate. Your decision may be based on several considerations.

## Planning for an Outdoor Party

An outdoor party is easier in many ways: easy cleanup, plenty of space, no rearranging of furniture or damage to the house. You'll need only to cut the grass to ready the site.

*But* . . .

- Will the weather cooperate? There's no guarantee, of course. You'll have to have an alternative plan for moving indoors. Can you move the picnic table to the basement or garage and continue the picnic party there? You might be able to schedule a rain date, but children will be very dis-

> We had a party for our 4-year-old in the gym of our local park. The kids brought trikes/bikes to ride while the parents rested between activities.
> *Karen Burkland, Sherman Oaks, CA*

appointed that the party they've been looking forward to has been postponed.

- Is your yard fenced so the party can be contained? If the fence is wooden, are there splinters or sharp points that can hurt children?

- Do you have a pool? Is it fenced so kids can't get to it unless you want them to, and will you have *lots* of helpers to watch them?

- Are there poisonous plants in your yard that toddlers might try to eat? Some dangerous ones are oleander, rhododendron, azalea, bittersweet, nightshade, and lily of the valley—yes, those beautiful bell-shaped flowers are toxic! Check also for mushrooms, as many types can be poisonous.

- Do you have a sprinkler system with pipes or spigots that kids might trip over?

## Planning for an Indoor Party

Don't wear yourself out cleaning the house or apartment. Straighten up for the adults a bit, but the children will never notice. Only your anxiety will show. And in a few hours you will only be doing it all over again!

- Confine the party to 1 or 2 rooms for optimum efficiency— one for eating, the other for activities. Childproof both rooms according to the ages of the children and, if necessary, move some furniture out of the activity room or push it up against the wall.

- Be firm about the physical limits of the party. Keep bedroom doors closed if they're on the way to the bathroom. Remove keys from doors; remove anything in the party area that's even remotely precious. Your main problems may be with "regulars," the kids who are already familiar with your house and feel at home there.

- Put away toys that won't be used for the party so they won't distract or tempt the guests.

- Tie streamers or place a safe, expandable gate (not the accordion-style) across the entrance to any room that doesn't have a door.

- Be sure to designate a place for the children to put their coats and a place to stash presents safely until they're opened. If you don't have a good spot for the gifts, a decorated laundry basket is nice and portable.

# Parties Away from Home

If you don't have your party at your home, you'll need to choose a restaurant or another spot for an outing. Partying outside your home has obvious advantages. You can come back to a clean house, a haven after an emotional and exhausting outing. But think *carefully* about it if you have children 4 or under. The danger in partying away from home with little children is that they will be difficult to manage and are likely to be overwhelmed by the excitement of an unfamiliar place. Parties for children 5 and up have a much better chance of succeeding away from home. The novelty of these types of parties also can lose their appeal after repetitive birthday trips to the same location.

But if your house or apartment is not suitable for a party, here are some ideas of places to go:

- a child-oriented restaurant

- a zoo

- a video/pizza parlor

- a library at preschool story hour

- a movie or children's show

- a hands-on museum

- a theme park

- a preschooler's gymnastic center

For older children, consider:

- bowling

- miniature golf

- roller skating

- ice skating

*Don't:*

- have a swim party (or any other activity that requires lots of adult supervision and can be truly dangerous).

- visit the planetarium (or any other place that requires the children to sit still and be quiet for any length of time).

- have the party at Grandma's. She should enjoy—not work!

## Fast-Food Chains

Many fast-food restaurants that specialize in hamburgers, pizza, and ice cream offer special rates and rooms for parties held in their establishment.

Be aware that two locations of the same franchise can be remarkably different. Sites that offer private party rooms and will make special arrangements can be discovered by talking to other parents and calling more than one location of a franchise and asking for a description of the party area and their services.

Call ahead in plenty of time to make reservations in a private room, if they offer one, or plan to be there at a time when you can have a corner to yourself.

Order the same thing for everyone, or offer only two options. Offering more choices will only lead to confusion.

When you call the restaurant, be prepared to ask very specific questions:

- What *exactly* is offered in the way of food, table decorations, favors, and activities, and at what cost?

- How long is the party expected to last?

- Are there suggested ages for the number of guests at the party?

- Is a minimum or maximum number of guests required?

- Does the birthday child get special recognition and attention?

---

## But Is It Worth It?

**Before you sign up for any fast-food restaurant, consider these parents' experiences:**

**The worst party I can remember was one for 3-year-olds at a pizza place. The children were terrified of the people dressed in animal costumes and clung to their moms.**

*Karen Dockrey, Burke, VA*

**The worst party we experienced was at a hamburger chain restaurant. The noise and confusion were awful. The birthday child seemed to get lost in the shuffle. And all this was topped off by poor food. Yuck!**

*Judi Hoey, Morristown, NJ*

**My children have not enjoyed parties at hamburger fast-food places where they were expected to behave and sit still. Both of my children prefer parties in people's houses with not too many children. The best one was outside!**

*Harriet Landry, Belford, NJ*

**I didn't keep track of how many kids my 4-year-old social butterfly had invited to McDonald's. I had to pay for all fourteen!**

*Karen Miller, Long Lake, MN*

---

Just to balance this account, it is necessary to report that half a class of Montessori preschoolers I interviewed preferred a party at a hamburger fast-food chain over a home party!

# Party Themes

Some parents find it easier to plan birthday parties if they start with a theme around which they can organize invitations, decorations, refreshments, and activities. Browsing through the party supplies at a card shop or department store will probably give you enough ideas for a dozen theme parties. Your child's favorite stories, interests, or songs can also spark your imagination. Or you can check with friends, relatives, and teachers for ideas.

Don't feel, however, that you *must* create a theme to build the party around. Remember, your party already has one theme: it's a birthday party.

Some traditional ideas for theme parties are briefly described in Chapter 10. Most are for children 3 and up. Don't go overboard with decorations and elaborately structured activities. Small children won't (really, can't) appreciate your efforts, and they may be overwhelmed by too much organization and your need to attend to peripheral details.

# Entertainers?

After you've considered the ages, interests, and attention spans of the children who will be at the party, you may decide that you want someone to come in and entertain them for a half-hour or so or run the party activities. Preschoolers have short attention spans, so a show should not be planned for more than 25 or 30 minutes. Consider entertainers who have been recommended by friends, relatives, or an agency. You can also check in the Yellow Pages or the newspaper classifieds.

For young children especially, don't let the entertainer be a surprise; it may prove to be terrifying rather than terrific. One mother attended a party that was going well until Superwoman suddenly (and unexpectedly) climbed over the backyard fence, scaring the 3-year-old guests.

Magicians can provide wonderful entertainment for kids,

but only if the children are old enough to understand the concept of magic—probably at 5 or 6.

## Hiring Considerations

- Everybody's favorite, the clown, can satisfy even quite small children if it's understood that he or she will put on a very brief show for toddlers and be available to circulate and entertain during the rest of the party. Ask your potential clown entertainer how he or she handles small children who have never seen or been close to a clown before. Some put on their costume as part of the act, in order not to frighten small children.

- Be sure the entertainer is used to working with children and will be able to handle outbursts or lack of attention.

- Ask for names and phone numbers of satisfied customers, then call them for references.

- Get all the details before you hire an entertainer. Some will provide favors, for example, and you need to know that ahead of time.

- Let the entertainer know about any potential problems that may arise with specific children, such as one who's handicapped or one who's afraid of animals, so he or she can adjust the show accordingly.

- And prepare the children for the type of entertainment they'll be seeing. Introduce your entertainer and tell the kids what kinds of things they'll be seeing and hearing.

Maybe you can get Dad into a Big Bird costume. You can also check with local high schools, colleges, and churches or your parks and recreation department to find out about aspiring young entertainers who will not charge as much as professionals and may do a wonderful job. You may even find a teenager in your neighborhood who puts on fine puppet shows.

## *Video Entertainment*

Home movie equipment has recently given way to VCRs. You can rent a VCR ($10 to $20 per day) if you don't own one, along with the tapes to show on it. A feature movie is too long for most young children's attention span, especially a group's worth! Shorts or cartoons are good choices. Remember that major library centers also have good selections of videotapes at less expensive rental rates.

> **The worst party we've encountered had a viewing of** *The Empire Strikes Back* **on a VCR. It was mayhem!**
> *Myra Weaver, Hollywood, FL*

# A Slumber Party?

Having 1 or 2 children sleep over can be a very special way to celebrate a birthday. The age and maturity of your child, as well as your child's friends, will be the significant factor in your decision. Perhaps your child's best friend is not yet ready to sleep away from home. This is not uncommon.

# A Surprise Party?

Surprise parties are rarely successful for children under the age of 12—half the fun for little children is the anticipation!

# Profit from Our Mistakes

The worst birthday parties I've given and attended were for children under 4. They're too young to appreciate being the honored one or being a guest. As hosts, they want to win all the games and keep all the prizes. As guests, they want to keep the presents for themselves. Parents tend to invite too many children for too many hours.

*Karen Gromada, Cincinnati, OH*

The *very* worst birthday party was the one I had for my 6-year-old (obviously my first child). We invited her entire first-grade class of 32. Pandemonium resulted, with all scheduled games played in half the time allotted, kids fighting all over the house, and screaming you wouldn't believe. My second child was allowed to invite only 6 kids to her sixth birthday party, and I think my third had 4.

*Kathryn Ring, Scottsdale, AZ*

I once made the mistake of inviting the mothers as well as the kids. I had a simple lunch planned for the children and an elaborate one for the mothers (buffet-style). There was no way I could keep both groups happy.

*Linda Phelps, Clarendon Hills, PA*

The worst birthday party was for a 4-year-old, attended by 2 children and 10 adult relatives. All I heard was, "Quiet down. Don't be so noisy." It wasn't even fun for me!

*Kathy Hickok, Delray Beach, FL*

# How Do I Make the Party Inviting?

Sometimes you may feel that you must invite certain children, more than you had wanted to, because you must reciprocate. Not true! You've got to plan a party that will work for your child.

You can invite the guests by phone or by mail, or you and your child can hand-deliver special invitations. Just *don't* plan to have a child hand out invitations at school, nursery school, or Sunday school, or you'll also be inviting all sorts of trouble, ranging from the loss of all the cards to the hurt feelings of children who aren't invited. Send out invitations 10 days or 2 weeks ahead, if possible.

## Invitations

Invitations are an important part of your party. They set the mood, tell what kind of party it will be, and help your child's anticipation get going. More often than not, we buy invitations (which the birthday child can help pick out), but you can also make them. Actually, this can be a fun project, especially if your child is old enough to help. Even the youngest child can put decorative stickers on invitation cards.

If your child's friends live in the neighborhood, you might have your child hand-deliver the invitations. If there is a theme, such as a circus party, have the birthday child dressed as a clown to deliver them.

If you choose to invite by phone, let your child extend the invitation to the guests if he or she wants to, but *you* follow up with a parent. Write down all the information before you start calling so you won't forget anything, and be very clear about the details.

## Homemade Invitations

- Buy plain postcards and let your child decorate them. You may wish to type the information neatly to save space.

- Use a recent photo of your child as a postcard, or, if you need all the space on the back for the information, slip the photo into an envelope.

- Cut birthday gift wrap or plain paper into clever shapes, a little smaller than the envelopes, and write all the information on the blank side. Good patterns for cutouts can be found in children's picture books or coloring books—trace on graph paper to enlarge easily if necessary.

- Decorate plain paper invitations with stickers, pictures cut from magazines, your child's drawings, or rubber stamp designs. Glue on sequins, buttons, or pieces of ribbon.

- Buy precut blank puzzles and write the information on them before you break them apart. Or make your own puzzles by writing on plain index cards and cutting them into several pieces.

- Blow up a balloon, put the invitation inside, and then let the air out. (It may be best to include slips of paper in the envelopes telling invitees to blow up and pop the balloons.) Or blow up the balloons, write the information on them with a ballpoint pen or marker, and then deflate the balloons, put in an envelope, and mail.

- Cut out strips of paper dolls, hearts, or other shapes and write the invitations on them, one item per figure.

- Photocopy a birth annoucement or birth certificate for the "cover" of the invitation. Party details can go on the back.

- Mail the party invitation with glitter or confetti inside so that it spills out when the invitation is opened.

- Let your invitation be connected to a party theme, if you are using one: a palette shape for an artists party; a beach party invitation can be written on a plastic shovel; a dinosaur shape can be traced around a dinosaur cookie cutters for a prehistoric party, or even write on the napkin from a fast-food restaurant you might decide will be the party location!

- Create a poem: "The time has come for birthday cake, It's my day for which we'll bake, A cake so glorious you will see, So please come over and share it with me."

---

## Specialized Invitations

Puzzled about where to get **blank puzzle notes** to spell out your message? They come in white but you can always spray paint and decorate them first before writing out the party information. If you can't find them at your local card shop, you can order them by mail from:

Bits and Pieces
1 Puzzle Place
Stevens Point, WI 54481
(1-800-JIG-SAWS)

Or you can use your home **computer** to create not only cards but banners, name tags, place mats, place cards, or award certificates. Available software is:

The Walt Disney Card and Party Shop
*Bantam Electronic Publishing*

The Print Shop
*Broderbund Software*

---

## Special Hand-Delivered Invitations

- Cupcakes, with invitations folded and "cornered" into the frosting.
- Boxes of animal crackers with invitations slipped inside.
- Decorated baskets, bags, or boxes with folded pictures, cutouts, or paper flowers inside with information written or typed on them.

## *Information to Include*

- *Whose party it is.* And be sure it's clear that it's a birthday party; nothing is worse than being the only one not to bring a gift because he or she *didn't know.* It also doesn't hurt to mention how old the birthday child will be—relatives especially may have a hard time keeping track.

- *Where the party will be.* If you think it's necessary or helpful, include a photocopied map to show how to get to your house.

- *The date and time of the party.* Remember, the ending time is as important as the beginning time. Don't forget to add that you'll be taking the children home, if that will be the case.

- *Special instructions,* such as, "Wear play clothes for an outdoor party," "Bring swimsuit," or "Bring highchair or infant seat and toddler's own bottle or cup."

- *What will be served:* lunch, supper, or just cake and ice cream.

- *Your request that parents accompany children,* if that's the case.

- *RSVP,* with your phone number and the date by which you need the answer. *Very important!!*

## *When the RSVPs Come In*

- Ask if there are food allergies or other problems you should know about and prepare for.

- Also be prepared to give gift suggestions to those who ask.

- Tell parents which other children are invited, so carpools can be arranged.

- And if someone doesn't call by the date requested, *you* call, just to be sure the invitation was received. You need to know who's coming, and so does your child.

---

### No-Shows

Guests have been known to fail to turn up because of a communicable illness, broken bone, transportation problems, a last-minute conflict of schedules, and sometimes, simple forgetfulness. Keep your sense of humor and a sense of perspective and you'll keep your friends, too.

---

# Party Countdown Plan

*2 Weeks Ahead:* Discuss plans with your child who is old enough to help make decisions. Check your camera, flash attachment, VCR, tape recorder, and any other equipment you intend to use to be sure it will work. This will give you a chance to send out anything requiring repair. Send invitations.

*1 Week Ahead:* Check off RSVPs received and call any parents who have not responded. Invite other guests if many originally invited cannot come. Buy or make decorations. Order cake. Get prizes, favors, and any supplies you'll need for activities, such as paper, scissors, and glue.

*3 Days Ahead:* Buy groceries. Pick up any chairs, tables, or props you'll be borrowing. Check out records or tapes from the library and try them out. Order the cake if you forgot to before or buy any ingredients needed to bake one.

*1 Day Ahead:* Bake the cake or pick one up from the bakery (hide it!); prepare any food you can. Wait—don't blow up the balloons yet, but do prepare loot or favor bags.

*5 Hours Ahead:* Finish the food preparation. Prepare room or yard, set up decorations. Pick up helium balloons or blow up regular ones. Put prizes and activities supplies near the spots where they'll be needed. Allocate time to fix yourself up before the party.

*1 Hour Ahead:* Help birthday child get dressed. Set up food and serving trays, set the table. Let your child help as much as possible.

# Let the Fun Begin

### That First Birthday Party

Let's be honest: your child's first birthday party is really for *you* and the family. Your hands will guide tiny ones in opening the presents, you will blow out the candles, and you will accept the congratulations. The party will not be meaningful for your 1-year-old, and you won't hurt his or her feelings if you choose to make it a celebration for adults only—really a celebration of the anniversary of your becoming a parent.

A 1-year-old will experience the atmosphere of the occasion and delight in the attention, but the concept of a party is not within his or her grasp. The birthday child of this age has been known to be far more intrigued with the boxes and wrapping paper than with the gifts.

If you do decide on a party with other children or babies present, you may wish to do the inviting by phone, because you'll have a lot of information to convey. Make it perfectly clear that at least 1 parent must accompany every child, and get across the idea that older children are not invited, if that's the case. Plan on a very short party, unless you have plenty of room and equipment so the babies can go to bed while the adults enjoy themselves. And childproof your play area carefully, remembering that it will probably contain both crawling and walking (staggering!) babies.

## Guests

- Make it clear that each parent is in charge of his or her own baby.

- Make it a BYO (Bring Your Own) _____* party, with the guests supplying their own *highchairs, walkers, bottles, or small chairs, as you wish.

- Be sure your child has some exposure to other people, including other babies, before the party so it doesn't come as too much of a shock.

## Refreshments

- Save the big cake for the adults and let the babies have an unfrosted cupcake to minimize the mess.

- Or go ahead and frost the cupcakes. Faces smeared with frosting do make wonderful photos and happy memories.

- Serve ice cream in small cones for easier eating for babies.

- Consider teething biscuits as appropriate treats (or wrapped, as party favors). Provide only chokeproof edibles.

- Place your child in a highchair at candle-blow-out time so he or she doesn't accidentally fall forward into the lighted candle.

- Put the children around a low table on small chairs or boxes, if they won't be in highchairs. And expect that there'll be lots of getting up and going to Mommy or Daddy.

- And skip the cute paper tablecloth and napkins; they're liable to be torn and eaten.

- Set up a salad or sandwich bar for adults so they can eat at their own convenience. Or be practical and supply only adult finger foods that can be eaten with a baby on one arm.

Activities to consider? Walker races; crawl to the $5 bill race; toy swap (ask each parent to bring one toy from home so the children can have the fun of a "new" toy to play with for the duration of the party).

For the first birthday, the thing you should be most generous with is film and flashes! Pictures will supply your child's only recollection of this first party.

---

## The Golden Birthday

This happens only once in a person's life. It is the birthday when the day of the month coincides with the chronological age. For example, if your birthday is on the fifteenth, your fifteenth birthday is your Golden Birthday.

---

# Timing of Activities

The basic segments of a birthday party after the first year are:

1. Guest arrival and beginning activity
2. Events, activities, and/or entertainment
3. Refreshments
4. Opening presents, distributing favors, and farewells.

Below are 2 loose schedules that may help you plan the timing of your party activities. Keep in mind that the time suggested for refreshments includes serving time; eating cake and ice cream takes only 5 minutes.

## A Party of 1 to 1½ Hours

1. Arrival: 10 minutes, with free play for those who come earliest. Set out a few toys suitable for the children's ages and have someone to supervise them and help them get acquainted or play cooperatively.
2. Open gifts: 15 minutes.
3. Refreshments: 10–20 minutes, for ice cream and cake.
4. Structured activities: 10–30 minutes for singing, story reading, games, crafts, etc., depending on the ages of the children.
5. Goodbyes: 10 minutes, as children are picked up or as you get them ready to be taken home. If they are being picked up, plan for free play while they wait. Don't have an exciting game that they'll hate to leave.

## A Party of 2 to 2½ Hours

1. Arrival: 15 minutes, with free play or a game or activity that newcomers can easily join when they arrive.
2. Special activity: 25–45 minutes, for a major crafts project or an entertainer.

3. Refreshments: 15–30 minutes, depending upon what you're serving.
4. A hunt: 5–10 minutes, which can be planned to take place before refreshments, or after, or as one of the games.
5. Games: 30 minutes, for anywhere from 3 to 7 games, either alternating between quiet and active ones, or having the quiet games at the end as you wind the children down for the next event.
6. Presents and goodbyes: 20–30 minutes, and parents who may arrive early can watch the gift-opening.

## Opening Activities

Do give some thought to this part of your party. Choose an activity that allows guests to join in as they arrive. Craft activities seem to work best. There are a good number to choose from starting on page 77. It can be as simple as having torn-out coloring book pages and crayons on a table, or making an edible necklace of licorice strings, or as ambitious as tracing the outline of the children's bodies on large paper as they arrive, which they can then color in.

---

As the children arrive, they take a seat around a large sheet of white paper. Each child designs a section, and it can be cut up and sent home with each child. You can have a theme, but it's not necessary.
*Linda Merry, St. Louis Park, MN*

---

# Setting the Stage for Party Manners

Naturally you'd like your birthday child to be a beautifully behaved, courteous host or hostess, more concerned about the guests' pleasure than about his or her own. Forget it. It won't happen for a good many years. Parties often bring out the worst in very young children—your own and the guests. Don't ruin the party for your child by prompting or scolding; this just isn't the time.

Talk about the party beforehand, though. We are so used to party traditions that we often forget to tell a 2- or 3-year old what to expect. It's a good idea to repeat the sequence of events and the rules you expect to be followed. You can try to get a few messages about manners across to all but the youngest of children. Just don't expect any finesse.

- Encourage your child to disguise his or her "me first" behavior at least to the extent of saying hello before grabbing the presents.

- Remind your child that he or she is expected to say hello and goodbye to each guest.

- Teach your child some nice things to say about identical presents. Try, "I wanted another one, anyway," or, "It's good to have two of these." If a present duplicates something the child already has, it's probably best to say nothing.

- Prepare your child ahead of time for the end of the party. Show by your example that we say goodbye at the door and say thank you for the present, even if we can't remember what it was. (See p. 108 for more thank-you tips.)

It's reasonable for a birthday to be one time when being "selfish" is okay. The birthday child should *not* be expected to share the gifts or to let others play with them.

## Party Music

Music can be a great addition to any birthday party. Use it in the background or during games that call for it, such as Musical Chairs or Statues. You can often change the pace of a party by changing the music.

- Play quiet music while the children are eating. It helps maintain a quiet mood.

- Check out special "happy birthday" records or tapes from the library or look for them in record stores. Some that are available use Sesame Street, Winnie the Pooh, and Raggedy Ann and Andy themes.

- Try a sing-along with familiar songs, perhaps as an opening activity or at the end of the party. If you or your spouse (or friend or neighbor) play the guitar, the children will enjoy such a personalized sing-along!

- Order a personalized Happy Birthday record or cassette sung by "Captain Zoom." Your child's name will be sung eight times. Send a self-addressed, stamped envelope to American Pro, 200 University Ave., Westwood, MA 02090, and ask for the list of available names. Or call (617) 329-2080. You can also order a personalized birthday tape for any name from Cake & Candle cassettes, Inc., 365 Winthrop St., P.O. Box 268, Winthrop, MA 02152, (617) 846-8831 for $7.50 plus $1.50 postage. Allow 3-4 weeks for delivery.

## Party Memories

Movies and videotapes are wonderful for recording all the action and excitement of a birthday party, but be sure to take some still pictures, too, for the family album. Many parents like to make up a separate album or scrapbook for each child's parties over the years, assembling the shots in the order in which they were taken. Consider including any of the following: a sample invitation, your child's place card, a few of the cards received, the menu, and a list of the games played.

Help a child of 4 or older start a party scrapbook. Use a three-ring notebook with both plain and lined paper and some heavy dividers with pockets. Ribbons, scraps of wrapping paper, an invitation, newspaper headlines from the big day, and snapshots can be pasted on the plain paper. Include an outline of the birthday child's hand, the list of guests, presents received, the party menu. Other important items can be written on lined, three-holed paper, and mementos like birthday cards and small favors can be saved in the pockets.

## Still Photos

- Consider getting an adult friend, a sitter, or spouse to take the pictures so you can devote yourself to the children. Yes, you can do it yourself, but you'll be spreading yourself pretty thin.

- Keep the pictures candid—no "freeze and smile!" photos.

- Use an instant camera for some of the pictures if you have one; you'll be able to make sure they're exactly as you want them. Try to be inconspicuous about taking them if you are not prepared to have the kids get too engrossed in watching the film develop.

- Purchase a collage frame and add a birthday photo each year. You can personalize it with Press-type. Under each photo indicate your child's age. You may also wish to put your child's name on it. (If the empty frames bother you, fill them with extra pictures from this year's party, and replace them next year.)

> Take pictures of the decorations, the cake, and the table *before* the party begins, while they're all still in one piece!

## *Motion Pictures and Videotapes*

- Check into borrowing or renting a videotape camera. As long as you have a VCR, you'll have a place to play it. Children are fascinated with both the "instant replay" of themselves and watching themselves from the years before.

- If you have a movie camera or video camera, use it. But keep in mind that it's the party that's important, not the film you're making. It's easy to get carried away, and it's important that you don't.

- Have another adult in charge of equipment who understands it should be used sparingly, unobtrusively, and with a sensitivity to children, who may be intimidated by it.

- Make an annual event of taking moving pictures. It's a wonderful way to chart children's growth from year to year.

- Tape the sounds of the party on a cassette to be played as you show silent home movies.

- If you have old motion pictures of family events, they can be transferred onto video cassettes fairly cheaply. They make wonderful family entertainment.

---

Never discourage girls or boys from wearing fancy party clothes. They love to be photographed in them, and fancy dress often helps to quell wild antics.

---

- Reserve one videotape to use only for birthday parties for each child. That way each child can take their own tape with them when they reach adulthood.

# Let Them Eat Cake . . . and Other Yummies!

## Chapter 5

What is a party to little kids *but* cake and ice cream? You may be able to skip some of the other elements of the perfect party, but never the refreshments. You can't go wrong if you serve only ice cream and cake. If your party is for very young children, don't hesitate to serve the food soon after they arrive.

Limiting sugar at birthday parties is a personal decision. Most of us tend to throw strict nutritional guidelines out the window for this annual event. It's hard to know if sugar alone really contributes to hyperactivity at a party because the party usually causes its own emotional high.

## The Cake!!

For children the cake *is* the party. Whether helping to select it or making it, serving it, eating it, or just admiring it, for them the cake has a way of becoming the focal point of the whole wonderful birthday ritual.

Obviously, the easiest way to produce the most lavish, gorgeous birthday cake the guests have ever seen is to call the best bakery in town and order it, baked and decorated to your specifications. For children old enough to appreciate this luxury, it may be worth the expense. Kids under 10 will be satisfied with almost anything as long as it's sweet, covered with plenty of frosting, and blazing with candles. In fact, if the frosting and candles are impressive enough, the quality of the cake will never matter. A plain, commercially made or cake mix variety with an icing chosen and applied by the birthday child can it-self be a birthday highlight.

Tradition plays a large part in birthday celebrations, and one of the oldest traditions is that the birthday child is entitled to the first piece of cake, and to his or her choice of which piece. That preference is usually one with a candle or a frosting flower on it. Actually, all of the guests would probably prefer a piece with a decoration, and you might take this into consider-ation when you're decorating or ordering the cake. Make the decorations as large as possible to cover as much of the cake as possible. Or you might have a separate plate for decorations, and add one to each piece of cake after you cut it.

The song that accompanies every birthday party and the one without which no party is complete is, of course, "Happy Birthday." Traditionally, this is sung when the cake is carried in or after the candles are lit and before they're blown out.

*HAPPY BIRTHDAY TO YOU*           (key of C)
  GG   A    G   C  B

*HAPPY BIRTHDAY TO YOU*
  GG   A    G   D  C

*HAPPY BIRTHDAY DEAR* _____
  GG   G   E   C     B   A

*HAPPY BIRTHDAY TO YOU!*
  FF   E    C   D  C

## Candle Power

Practice makes perfect. A 2-year-old will enjoy learning and singing "Happy Birthday" prior to the party. The other skill to practice is how to blow out candles. Use a straw to explain the technique if your child can't copy your mouth movements.

- Remember that lighted candles can be dangerous. Watch bows and ruffles, and be aware that a little girl's long hair can catch fire if she leans too close to the candles to blow them out.

- Look for a special "12-year candle" that you can use over and over as a special tradition.

- For a dramatic effect, darken the room just before bringing in the lit birthday cake.

## Cake Concoctions ·

Perhaps you have a favorite cake recipe (or one your mother made for you as a child). White, yellow, or angel food cakes are usually safe choices with children. Carrot cake with a cream cheese frosting and iced zucchini bread are more nutritious choices, but children who have never tasted any kind of cake but yellow, white, or chocolate may refuse to eat anything unfamiliar. It's usually best to stick with the tried-and-true for birthday cakes if you have no special dietary concerns. If you are making from scratch a cake you haven't made before, do a practice run a week or so before. Nothing is more frustrating than having a cake not turn out to your satisfaction when you have all the other party details to attend to.

If you want to be a bit daring, consider one of these popular variations on the traditional cake:

- Make an ice cream cake by unwrapping a block of ice cream and covering it with lady fingers or other cookies. Return it to the freezer until ready to serve.

- Serve a platter of cupcakes with decorations and candles blazing. The advantages--"precut," easy-to-serve, all portions the same size--are obvious!

- Make a rainbow cake by dividing a white cake batter into thirds and adding a different food coloring to each for a three-color layered cake. Spread into separate pans and bake according to directions. Use frosting as a filler between each layer.

- Cut a sheet cake into generous serving-size rectangles. Frost and decorate to resemble a train.

- Before cutting a sheet cake into an unusual shape (such as a dinosaur), freeze it. To prevent additional crumbling when frosting sides, first brush edges with some preserves.

- Make a "ghosty" cake by baking your batter in a gingerbread cake pan and finishing it with white frosting.

- Create a "party favor" cake as follows: score a small, flat cake into 2-inch squares. Turn it upside down and scoop out some cake every 2 inches or so with a melon scoop. Plastic wrap a tiny toy and insert one in each hole. Turn the cake back over, frost and mark scored sections with a knife. When ready to serve, tell each child their piece of cake will have a hidden, non-edible surprise!

- Make cake cones by filling flat-bottomed ice cream cones half-full with the cake batter of your choice and place them on a cookie sheet or in a muffin tin. Bake according to directions for cupcakes. Decorate them yourself or let the party guests get involved.

For an unusual but fun cake you might want to try:

### Birthday Popcorn Cake

6 qts. popped popcorn
1 lb. gumdrops
1 1/2 cups peanuts
1 large bag of
   marshmallows
1/2 cup salad oil
1/4 cup margarine

Combine popcorn, gumdrops and peanuts in bowl. Melt together marshmallows, oil and margarine over low heat and mix together well. Pour this over the popcorn mixture and mix well. Press into a well greased angel food cake pan. Cool 10 minutes. and remove from pan. Decorate to fit your needs.

### Party Cake Cookbook

Contains party theme ideas, recipes, and more. Oriented for school-age years but has lots of good ideas.

Better Homes & Garden
   Books®
Available wherever books
are sold.

## Frosting

Kids *do* judge a cake by its cover--the frosting. They don't care about nutrition, and they seldom eat enough of any topping for it to matter. You can make frosting from scratch or buy it by the package or can.

Freeze the cake or cupcakes before frosting them. The cake will be easier to work with and the frosting will harden faster on a cold cake.

## *The Guest-Decorated Cake*

If the party guests are at least 4 or 5 years old, and if there aren't too many of them, you may wish to let them help the birthday child decorate the cake. Buy or make a plain sheet cake and frost it with white icing. Then supply several tubes of different colored frosting for the guests. Write decorating ideas on small slips of paper ("Write Happy Birthday," "Write Mary's name," "Make a border around the cake," "Add flowers") and have each child make one addition to the cake. If only one child at a time will be able to work on the cake, have the others work simultaneously at decorating a paper table-cloth or place mats with crayons.

Another do-it-yourself delight is decorating birthday cup-cakes or cake cones as either an early activity or just before eating them. Hand out wooden Popsicle sticks for easy frosting. Divide prepared frosting among small bowls. Add a few drops of different food coloring to each, along with flavorings like peppermint, lemon, or orange. Then provide fun toppings: sugar sprinkles, animal crackers, gumdrops, carob or chocolate chips, M&M™ Chocolate Candies, red hots, and such.

## *Easy Frosting and Decorating Tidbits*

- Sprinkle a cake or cupcakes still hot from the oven with chocolate chips. As they soften, spread with a flat knife for a quick and easy frosting. Let cool before eating.

- Before frosting, slip pieces of waxed paper under the cake on all sides to protect the serving plate. When the cake is frosted, slide the papers out, and there'll be no drips or splatters on your plate.

- Use big gumdrops, marshmallows, or Lifesavers© for candle holders on the cake.

- Set a small glass of flowers, real or artificial, in the center of a tube cake.

- Decorate the top of the cake or cupcakes with plastic miniatures that complement whatever party theme you have chosen.

- Color the frosting your child's favorite color, even if it looks a bit outrageous.

- Create a balloon bouquet design on a cake by using licorice whips and pastel mint wafers on a frosted cake.

- After frosting a rectangular or square cake, use red string licorice and put it on the cake to resemble a tied package. Place a bow in the center.

- Use cookie cutters to imprint patterns in frosting and then outline the designs with tube frosting.

## Ice Cream Serving Suggestions

Offer one kind of ice cream. Vanilla is probably your best bet unless you know you have a group of chocolate lovers. Others get around this by buying Neapolitan ice cream that has three flavors combined (vanilla, chocolate, and strawberry). Little kids don't eat the exotic.

Homemade ice cream can be exciting for children over the age of 4, but only if you have the equipment and have done it before. Timing is important. You may have to start freezing the ice cream before the party starts to ensure its being ready to eat before the guests leave.

- Consider serving ice cream in cones for easier handling. Or make ice-cream clowns, with the cone mounted on the scoop as the hat and facial features added to the ice cream.

- Put a miniature marshmallow or two in the bottom of a pointed cone, or put a large marshmallow or small cookie in a flat-bottomed cone to keep ice cream from leaking and to make a surprise treat at the end. A more nutritious alternative—use a slice or two of banana.

- Or scoop the ice cream into paper cups or cupcake papers and keep them in the freezer until you have cut and served the cake. Variation: roll the scoops in colored or chocolate "jimmies" before freezing.

- Or buy vanilla dixie cups—wooden spoons and all!

- Put a candle in each child's ice cream scoop (or cupcake) so everyone gets to blow one out. Be sure the birthday child blows his or hers out first.

## Planning the Other Refreshments

Are you going to serve a meal? It's not necessary, but it will keep children seated and occupied for longer than it takes to eat just ice cream and cake.

Keep in mind as you plan that the refreshments will be eaten—or *not* eaten—by *children*—and probably finicky ones at that! If you decide to extend yourself and serve lunch or supper (best reserved for kids at least 4 or over), remember that this is not the time to try out the new quiche recipe or make tacos. Avoid messy foods like spaghetti or anything in gravy or sauce. The exception is Kraft's Macaroni and Cheese, which seems to be the all-time favorite.

Remember the cardinal rule: Keep it simple!

Choose foods that can be prepared ahead of time; avoid any that require last-minute preparation.

Snacks during activities will distract the kids, and you'll probably have extra mess to clean up. Save all food for the table.

If you are on a limited budget, don't serve a meal. Cake and ice cream are all that's really needed.

## Menu Ideas

Stick to the foods children like and can handle easily, even if the meal doesn't seem very festive to you: hot dogs (for older children only due to choking hazard), hamburgers, pizza, peanut butter and jelly sandwiches, cheese cubes, vegetable sticks with a dip, and fruit are all fine. The fewer pieces of silverware you need on the table, the easier your lunch or supper will be for the kids—and therefore for you.

### Sandwiches, Slightly Different

- Make up a platter of small peanut butter and jelly sandwiches cut into triangles. (No crusts, please. After all, this is a party!)

- Or cut traditional sandwiches with cookie cutters to make, for example, bunny- or heart-shaped sandwiches.

- Spread peanut butter on equal numbers of circles and triangles of bread. Then make clown faces by arranging a triangle hat next to each circle face. Decorate the face with jam, raisins, maraschino cherries, and coconut.

## A Birthday Sandwich

Make hero sandwiches with cold meats, egg or tuna salad, cheese—whatever you like. Poke holes in the crust and insert birthday candles. Serve tomato slices, lettuce, mayonnaise, pickles, and other additions on the side.

- Serve open-faced grilled cheese on bagels or on bread cut with cookie cutters.

- Make miniature easy-to-handle pizzas on English muffin halves, using any kind of topping you wish. Or serve small frozen pizzas.

- Serve hamburgers on tiny cocktail buns. Or shape small hamburgers and place them between flattened-out refrigerator biscuits, crimped together around the edges to keep the meat inside, and bake them according to package directions for biscuits (approximately 20 minutes). Add a dollop of catsup or barbecue sauce to each before putting together and crimping.

- To make pigs-in-a-blanket wrap weiners in strips of refrigerated crescent roll dough, patted out flat. Bake in the oven at 400° or roast over coals outdoors. If the kids will be roasting their own, make "shields" against the heat by poking the ends of the roasting sticks through foil pie plates before putting the weiners on them.

### Other Lunch and Supper Ideas

- Make whole meal kabobs on Popsicle sticks, using cubes of cheese, cold meat, or ham; melon balls or pineapple chunks; and cherry tomatoes, pieces of green pepper, or other vegetables you think the kids might eat.

A super treat for kids to make for themselves is peanut butter roll-ups. Smash one slice of bread with a
rolling pin. Spread with peanut butter (add jelly,
wheat germ, peanuts, anything you like). Roll up like
a jelly roll and cut off half-inch slices. Pop into mouth
and smack lips.

*M. Van Dan, Hebron, IL*

- Make a "Happy Birthday" salad by hollowing out the inside of a watermelon and filling it with fruit. Replace the
top of the melon and insert candles into holes in the rind.

- Serve tuna or egg salad in ice cream cones for easy eating.

- Put a small serving of cottage cheese on a bed of shredded
lettuce for each child. Decorate the cheese as a face with
carrot or celery pieces for ears, a peach slice for a smile, an
olive for a nose, raisins for eyes, and julienne celery for
whiskers.

- Oven-fry small chicken drumsticks or wings, or buy
cooked frozen chicken pieces and heat them up, and supply dips for them—sweet and sour sauce, barbecue sauce,
or plain catsup.

- Stuff celery with peanut butter, cream cheese, American
cheese spread, or tuna salad.

- Let each child have his or her own small bag of chips to
prevent grabbing and fighting over who got more.

## Time to Eat

- Always seat the children and *bring the food to them!* You can
have an attractive, convenient buffet table in a few years

when the kids are old enough to serve themselves and carry loaded plates.

- Try to have the correct size table and chairs for little people.

## . . . And to Drink

- Don't serve beverages that stain (grape juice, for instance).

- The juices in small cartons, with straws inserted in tiny holes, are favorites and are almost spill-proof, and they save you the trouble of cups or glasses. Try apple juice, lemonade, or cranapple juice instead of less nutritious drinks.

- Offer "rainbow" milk. Have two or more pitchers of milk to which you've added different food coloring and perhaps a drop of vanilla.

- A small amount of cranberry juice mixed with lemonade makes pink lemonade.

- Mix sherbet and ginger ale to make a punch that fizzes.

- Don't pour the drinks ahead of time at the table. First make sure each child is settled in a chair and ready to hold on to his or her cup. Fill cups only one-third full to avoid major spills. Or fill them in another room to bring in on a tray after everyone is seated.

- Remember that water also quenches thirst.

## Other Nuts and Bolts

- Don't serve nuts or hard candies to children 3 and under. They might choke. Beware, too, of hot dogs, as they are a leading cause of choking in young children.

- For children over 3, use a mixture of shelled peanuts, raisins, and M&M™ Chocolate Candies to fill nut cups if you feel they're necessary.

- Hand out wrapped popcorn balls or pretzels tied with a ribbon as take-home favors.

- Dried fruit rolls are popular additions to the table or favor bag. Tying a ribbon around them makes them special.

- To make finger Jell-O™, dissolve 2 envelopes of unflavored gelatin in 1 cup of cold water and add 1 6-ounce package of flavored gelatin to 1 cup of boiling water. Combine and add ½ cup of cold water. Chill in a lightly greased pan until solid. Use cookie cutters to make fancy shapes to complement your theme.

- Wherever possible, use paper and plastic. The added expense is well worth the savings in cleanup time and worry about breakage.

- Pour out any liquid left in cups, then wrap up all the paper plates, cups, and garbage right in your paper tablecloth, and throw it all away. Have several large, heavy-duty plastic trash bags handy.

---

Even if you watch your child's diet carefully throughout the year, taking care that no junk food ever passes his lips, this is the one day you ought to relax your restrictions. Console yourself that those sugary treats are an indulgence only once a year. I've had very bad luck with carrot sticks, sunflower seeds, and my nutritious no-sugar munchies at kids' parties. The guests protested loudly, and the birthday child was very disappointed.

*Mary McNamara, Wayzata, MN*

- Expect small children to eat very little. It won't be because your refreshments aren't delicious but because the children will be too excited to bother with food. Make portions small. You can always serve seconds.

- Plan something for fast eaters to do when they've finished. It's too much to expect kids to sit quietly at the table waiting for dawdlers.

- Or plan to read to the children while they eat, to keep everyone content.

# Special Menus

If your child suffers from diabetes, lactose intolerance, or food allergies, or is on a special diet for hyperactivity or another problem, you'll undoubtedly plan the party refreshments around his or her requirements. If the parent of a guest who has such problems offers to send along suitable food, accept gratefully. You can offer non-diet foods to the other children if you wish, but be prepared to watch to be sure the restricted child eats only what's allowed.

## Ice Cream Substitutes

Several milk- and butterfat-free "ice creams" are now available. One is called Tofutti; check your supermarket or ice cream store for others. They look like ice cream, they taste like ice cream, and the chances are good that only you will know the difference. Other alternatives are fruit ices, sorbets, or Italian ices. They're colorful and tasty enough to appeal to kids. Be aware that most sherbet you buy in stores does contain milk.

## Watermelon Sorbet

6 cups ripe watermelon, cut
  up and seeded
1 cup sugar
juice of ½ lemon

Blend watermelon with sugar
in blender or food processor.
Add lemon juice and stir well.

Spoon mixture into an ice cube
tray and freeze for 1½ hours.
Remove and beat until
smooth; return to freezer for
several hours or overnight.
Serve in small bowls and decorate with watermelon balls, if
desired. Serves 4 to 6.

## Milk-Free Ice Cream

1 (8 oz.) container Richwhip®
  topping (or any nondairy
  equivalent frozen whipped
  topping)
¼ cup sugar, or equivalent
  sweetener
1 teaspoon vanilla
optional: 1 mashed banana,
  1 cup berries or other fruit

Whip the topping as you
would heavy cream. When

thickened, add sugar, vanilla,
and fruit (pureed or whole).
Freeze for ½ hour. Remove
and beat for 1 minute. Pour
into a storage container, cover,
and freeze. Natural it is not
(read the ingredients listed on
the topping carton), but milk-
free and delicious it is! This
mixture, if pureed well, can be
used in an ice cream maker.
Serves 4.

## Banana/Carob Milk-Free Ice Cream

6 ripe bananas
3 tablespoons honey or sugar
⅓ cup oil
2 tablespoons carob powder
4 tablespoons powdered soy
  milk
½ cup water

Blend all ingredients and
freeze. Serves 6 to 8.

If you haven't checked out your guests for possible allergies, you can use the following recipe (known to some as Crazy Cake) for an easy, good-tasting cake that avoids milk and egg allergens:

### Diplomatic Cake (Milk-Free and Egg-Free)

1 cup sugar
1½ cups flour
3 tablespoons cocoa or carob
   powder
1½ teaspoons baking soda
5 tablespoons salad oil
1 tablespoon vinegar
1 teaspoon vanilla
1 cup cold water

Combine dry ingredients, then pour in oil, vinegar, vanilla, and water, mixing well. Bake in 8 x 8 pan at 350° for 35–40 minutes. Frost or add icing after cake is cooled. Serves 6 to 8.

Here's another recipe for special diets:

### The Gluten-Free Birthday Cake

Buy a loaf of heavy rice bread, which looks like pound cake. Make butter frosting with hot water; butter, margarine, or soybean margarine; and confectioners' sugar. For coloring, use hot cranberry juice or hot grape juice. Because the bread is dry, extra frosting is needed.

## *Other Treats*

- Frozen bananas on a stick covered with honey or peanut butter and dipped in crushed nuts or seeds

- Carob chips

- Parfaits layered with yogurt, berries, peanut butter, and granola

- Fruit salads

- Cantaloupe boats: Construct a sailboat by putting cheese (sails) on pretzel sticks or wooden sticks (masts) on a small wedge of cantaloupe. Fill the cantaloupe with grapes, and put the sticks in among the grapes.

---

My 2-year-old, who is very sensitive to gluten and most fresh fruits and vegetables, has been to two parties. For the first, I brought a loaf of banana rice bread with pink frosting. As it turned out, she ate potato chips the whole time—the cake situation didn't bother her. For the second party, I made Jell-O™ mold and frosted it with colored whipping cream. It was a success, but she was most impressed by a few tastes of white frosting from the gluten cake. In both cases, I was more upset than she.

*Karen Haynes, Albuquerque, NM*

---

# Creating the Party Magic: Decorations, Favors, and Prizes

Decorations are the magic that transforms your home and separates your child's day from all the others to say, "You're special!"

But you don't have to spend a lot of money to create a party mood. Yes, stores offer wonderful party decorations, but indulge in them only if your budget allows. Inexpensive or homemade decorations can be just as festive. Whether you buy or make them, let your child help as much as possible.

## Decorative Materials

- Crepe paper for streamers

- Inexpensive posters

- Your collection of stuffed animals and dolls

- Buy or make your own confetti (it's a great way to keep a child busy with a hole puncher—use colored paper, leftover gift wrap, even aluminum foil). Confetti dresses up any table for children over the age of three who are no longer tempted to put it in their mouths. And it vacuums up easily.

# Balloons by Mail

Buy 10 personalized "Happy Birthday" balloons for your birthday boy or girl. Specify "stem down" if you're using helium or "stem up" if you are blowing them up yourself. Print your child's name clearly, and send your order with $3.49 plus $1.95 for postage (item #RP 121 1) to:

> Miles Kimball
> 41 West 8th Avenue
> Oshkosh, WI 54906

In their attractive catalog which features a complete line of children's party supplies, you will find balloons that tie into party themes. They also carry large, 12-inch balloons imprinted with a Happy Birthday greeting and your child's age (specify age from 1 to 12). Each package contains 6 latex balloons in assorted colors for $2.50 plus $1.75 for postage on orders up to $8. To receive a catalog or to order write:

> Everything But The Cake
> 607 Corona Street, Suite 272
> Denver, CO 80218-3406
> (303) 778-6228

And for a do-it-yourself "Happy Helium Balloon Kit" (20 3" balloons and enough helium in an aerosol-type can to inflate them), send $14.95 plus $4.25 for postage (item #71289) to:

> Edmund's Scientific
> 101 E. Glouster Pike
> Barrington, NJ 08007
> (609) 547-3488

## Balloons

Balloons—lots of them—are musts for children's birthday parties, and fortunately, they're not necessarily expensive. Use
dozens of them in all sizes, shapes, and colors, and look for
some that have your child's name printed on them.

- Get out the old bicycle pump to make blowing up easier.
  Or pick up an inexpensive push pump at the variety store
  (usually stocked next to the balloons). Stretch balloons
  first to make them easier to inflate.

- Don't buy helium balloons till party day. Some lose their
  "holding" power in a day.

- Expect some balloons to pop, so buy plain ones in quantity
  instead of in small packages. Do be careful to keep small

---

### Warning

Swallowed or inhaled balloons or pieces of balloons
present a serious suffocation threat. Be sure the
children play with only inflated, intact balloons.
Immediately dispose of any that break.

---

pieces of popped balloons away from toddlers, who might put them in their mouths and choke.

- To simplify cleanup, let the kids take balloons home as favors.

## Table Decorations

Remember that the less crowded the table the better. A too-large centerpiece and a lot of small items scattered about will produce spills in direct proportion to the inexperience and youth of the guests. You can attach bowls to the table with double-stick tape to keep them from tipping over.

### Centerpieces

- Attach a bunch of helium-filled balloons to the center of the table, adjusting them to float high enough so children can see across the table. Metal washers from the hardware store tied to the string of a floating balloon will "anchor" it to the table, if you prefer a balloon by each place setting. Or you can tie or tape one or two to the back of each chair.

- Use your cake as the centerpiece. Setting it on a pedestal (even a sturdy box covered with foil) will enhance its magic. Its beauty will be appreciated more if it's seen for longer than the few minutes before the candles are blown out and the cake is cut and eaten. Remove the cake to light the candles, and bring it back for the "Happy Birthday" song. If the cake is within reach of the guests, expect fingerprints and "taste marks."

- Set a big, pretty basket on the table and fill it with small balloons, popcorn balls wrapped in plastic wrap and tied with bright yarn, little house plants that will go home with the guests as favors, tiny stuffed animals, or anything pertaining to the party theme.

- Attach streamers to a light fixture over the table and run them to the edges of the room to make a canopy. Hang a mobile or a bunch of balloons from the center of the fixture.

- Dress up stuffed animals (a large one or several small ones) with party hats and streamers. Or follow your party theme when outfitting them.

---

### Paper Party Products by Mail

No time for shopping around or no good stores around you for party goods? Both of these companies offer a large selection of party items. Just looking through the catalogs can give you ideas to help you decide what kind of party you want to give.

The Party Basket, Ltd.
734 Nashville Avenue
New Orleans, LA 70115
(504) 899-8126
Free catalog on request

Paradise Products
Box 568
El Cerrito, CA 94530
(415) 524-8300
Send $2 for catalog

---

## Table Toppings

- Buy a plain white paper tablecloth that can be colored in advance by the birthday child or by the guests when they arrive. Or cover the table with plain, heavy paper and let little ones scribble with crayons as they wait to be served.

- Be sure any tablecloth has a short drop and will not rest on the laps or knees of the children.

- Use the colored comic sections of your newspaper taped together to make a colorful and inexpensive decorative table cover.

- Use a plain white tablecloth on which preschoolers can write their names. Later, embroider the names and use the cloth year after year, adding new names and repeating old ones.

- Design a place mat and photocopy it. Let your imagination run wild. Start with a picture of your child and let him or her embellish it with pictures or squiggles. Copy on colored paper, let your child add more color with crayons, and cover the mats with clear contact paper.

- Supply colored construction paper for place mats, with crayons for the children to decorate them. The color may bleed onto the tablecloth if the paper gets wet, but it will wash out with no problem.

- Or buy solid-color vinyl place mats that children (5 and over) can decorate with permanent markers or stickers and take home as party favors. (Be sure your table is protected if you use permanent markers.) Or offer crayons and washable markers if you want to keep the place mats.

- Let colorful napkins perk up the table if you're using plain white paper plates.

- Use a small blanket as a table pad if you are worried about water damage to a dining room table.

## Party Hats

Party hats, made or bought, are part of the birthday party tradition that children have come to expect. Besides, they help provide terrific party photos.

They may stay on for a long time or a short time. Age, comfort, and sophistication all play a part here. Yet all are loved at party time and as a take-home favor.

- Roll a rectangular piece of colored 8 x 12 construction paper into the shape of a cone and tape and/or staple shut. Trim as needed.

- Cut a zigzag pattern lengthwise across the middle of colored construction paper. Tape ends together to form a crown headband.

- Decorate a strip of sturdy paper to be used as an Indian headband, or attach small balloons for a fun party hat.

- Buy simple party hats and let the children decorate them with feathers, glitter, bows, fake flowers, and such.

- Make ties to go under the chin from party ribbon, string, or long, substantial rubberbands that can be cut and knotted after running through the two side holes in the hat.

## Place Cards

Use place cards even if the children are too young to read them. Everybody will want to sit by the birthday child, and place cards lend an air of authority that will avoid trouble.

Consider making name tags for each guest, too. They make children feel important and may be helpful to you, too, when you forget a child's name.

- Tie helium balloons with names written on them to the backs of the chairs.

- Write names on cutouts of gingerbread boys, paper dolls, animals—whatever suits your theme—and set them on the plates.

- Make paper cones of half-circles of heavy paper, taped or stapled together. Decorate with markers and stand, broad end down, with a lollipop in the center of each.

## *Table Settings as Place Cards*

- Write the children's names with permanent markers on paper cups or, better, on hard plastic cups or glasses, which will be less apt to tip.

- Write names on cutout paper shapes, punch holes at the tops and bottoms and weave drinking straws through them. Stick the straw ends into drinking cups or cupcakes.

- Use a paper tablecloth or an old white sheet and write the children's names on it at their places. Let older kids decorate the space around their names with crayons, perhaps as an arrival activity. Cover the names and drawings with brown paper and iron gently (be sure there's adequate padding on the table under the cloth) until the wax melts and lifts, leaving just the color.

- Use solid color paper plates and write the children's names around the edges.

## *Food as Place Cards*

- Make a place card necklace from sugar cookies (refrigerator cookies from the supermarket will do nicely) or plain rectangular biscuit cookies. Cut in shapes, if you like, and before baking make holes at the top for string. Write each child's name in frosting and string yarn through the hole.

- Or make cookie puzzles. Make the cookies fairly large; score lines for the pieces while they're warm, and break at divisions when they cool. Put them back together and write a child's name on each one.

- Or write the kids' names with squeeze-bottle honey on cookies and sprinkle with colored sugar.

- Turn sugar cones upside down and write names on them in frosting. Use the cones later for serving ice cream.

- Put small toys or candies in plastic sandwich bags, then into the toilet tissue cores you've saved for just such an occasion. Wrap the rolls in crepe paper, twist and tie at the ends. Write the children's names on the outside with markers.

- Fill small brown bags with candy and favors for each child. Fold over the tops (and staple or tape shut, if you wish) and write the names on the outsides of the bags—Presto! Party bags, ready to go.

- Make or buy hats and write names on them.

- Serve each child's food on a clean new Frisbee® that has his or her name written around the outside edge. Use paper plate liners to save yourself the trouble of cleaning the Frisbees before they go home with the kids.

## Place Cards to Use in Games or Activities

- Embroider or mark the names on beanbags, which will be used for a tossing game.

- Write the names on sandbox pails and shovels if there will be outdoor sandbox play after refreshments—and then send them home as favors.

- Or write names on small clay pots that hold plastic bags of soil and a few seeds each. After the refreshments, the children can plant the seeds.

# Decorating Indoors

You need not decorate more of the house than the play area and the room where the food will be served. Decorating the front door, however, helps set the party mood.

- Rub balloons against your clothes to create static electricity, and they will stick to walls by themselves.

- Tie crepe paper streamers or place a decorated, expandable gate across the entrance to any room that doesn't have a door.

- Attach streamers to the walls and ceiling with dabs of toothpaste—it will hold them nicely and it washes right off.

- Or try attaching streamers and inexpensive posters to painted walls with small dabs of rubber cement. It will roll up and rub off easily.

- Make paper mobiles by attaching cutouts to streamers at different lengths.

- Or make mobiles on coat hangers, with small dolls, cars, or other little toys. Remember to hang them at different lengths.

- Let preschoolers make streamers of paper chains they put together themselves.

- Draw theme art on posterboard for each child to color at the beginning of the party. Hang posters up for decorations, then send them home as a party favor.

- Dress up your collection of stuffed animals or dolls with party hats and streamers.

- Save decorations if they can be used again for another party.

## Decorating Outdoors

- Tie balloons to the doorway or mailbox to provide a festive air and to help guests find the house.

- Stretch a "Happy Birthday" banner across the front of the

house or above the front door. It can be made from a roll of drawing paper or an old sheet, or purchased in a gift store.

- Make a path from the front door to the party area, with arrows pointing the way to the "Fairy Castle," the "Dragon's Lair," or "Raggedy Ann and Andy's House." For extra emphasis, make footprints from construction paper for the kids to follow.

- String crepe paper streamers between bushes and trees to confine activities to appropriate areas.

- Hang thin ribbons of various colors from the lower branches of trees for a delicate, festive effect.

- Wrap crepe paper streamers around tree trunks to resemble candy canes.

- Tie balloons in bunches to trees and shrubs.

- Fasten bright posters to trees in the yard.

## Party Favors

Favors are definitely called for, at every age. Just be sure they're alike in size, color, and appeal, to avoid conflict. Let your child help you choose and make the favors. The "party bag" has become an accepted part of birthdays, it seems, so you may want to put together identical bags for everyone. Favors are fun to fit around your theme, which makes them even better souvenirs of your party.

Do not think kids won't like homemade favors—they appreciate any and all take-home items. And don't let fancy favors turn into a competitive item for you among your own peers.

Remember, when it comes to prizes, gifts, and possessions in general, preschoolers are self-centered, not selfish. There is a difference. *It is natural not to want to share at that age*. Selfishness involves understanding and rejecting the perspective of someone else. That's not the case with small children. They keep something to themselves because they do not fully understand the wishes or needs of others. And a birthday party is not the place to try to teach children how to share!

### Favors and Party Bags

- Avoid blowers. Children tend simply to blow them in each other's faces.

- Don't forget to supply identical party favors or party bags for the birthday child.

- Take an instant picture of each youngster with the birthday child as a take-home favor. If you don't have access to an instant camera, borrow one, or use your regular camera and mail the picture with an after-party thank-you note.

> **One of the most popular favors we ever gave out were live goldfish. We included a small bowl with gravel, food, etc. We got the idea from our party theme, which was fishing.**
> *Leslie Melamed, Deephaven, MN*

- Hand out the party bags at the *very end* of the party, as each guest is going out the door, and make sure they're marked with the children's names.

- Or wrap identical favors and put them in a big bag or box and use the "grab bag" method.

- Tape or staple to each favor an instant picture you've taken of each child, and let the kids find their own favors that way.

- Place an open gift-wrapped box on the party table as a centerpiece. Place a favor for each child inside, with a streamer tied to the favor and leading to each child's place at the table. Before serving the food, let each child pull the streamer to receive the attached favor.

## Favors to Buy

Any of the following are enjoyed by party-goers and should be gentle on your budget: Magic Slate™, jump ropes, animal crackers, pinwheels, crayons, markers, activity or coloring books, flashlights, novelty erasers, stickers, yo-yos, bubble blowers, miniature cards, magnets, plastic games, puzzles, key chains, to name a few!

- Whistles threaded with colorful shoelaces to be worn as necklaces.

- Fill party bags with wrapped candy (five kinds of small candies is ideal), a box of animal crackers, sugarless gum. Pens made to look and smell like candy give a sugarless favor "candy" overtones.

- Save shopping time and probably a little money by buying 4- or 6-pack sets of items such as clay sets, small cars, or other little items and dividing them among the bags.

- Buy (or make) modeling clay and place in individual plastic bags. Tie three bags together with a piece of yarn. The children can play with the clay at the party or take it home. Add a cookie cutter for even more fun.

---

# Party Favors by Mail

The following companies sell a wide variety of small, inexpensive party favors.

**M & N International, Inc.** Ask for the free "Party and
13860 West Laurel Drive   Promotions Book" catalog.
Lake Forest, IL 60045
(708) 680-4700

**Rewards Unlimited**    This catalog is filled with
PO Box 12456         distinct and unique stickers
Omaha, NE 68112       and novelties at economical
Free catalog.        prices. $10 minimum order.

**Stocking Fillas**     Their Party Club annual
1491 Sheridan Drive     catalog is filled with small
Buffalo, NY 14217      toys, presents and novel-
(416) 621-6100        ties. It is free on request.

---

## *Favors You Can Create*

- Make sticker books by stapling together several sheets of waxed paper and putting one sticker on each page. The stickers can be reused and moved from page to page.

- Personalize wide barrettes with tiny self-stick letters, or decorate them with small stickers.

- Decorate edges on an inexpensive picture frame with stickers, or personalize frames with permanent markers. An "instant" picture from the party can go home in it.

- Roll up several pages from a "just-add-water-and-paint" coloring book, tie with a ribbon, and attach a paintbrush.

- Weave ribbon through plastic strawberry baskets to hold favors. Add a handle made of pipe cleaners. These baskets can also serve as table decorations.

## Prizes: Yes or No?

If your birthday child is a toddler, you probably won't want to include prizes as part of the celebration—the children are too young for real games and usually aren't able to handle the idea of someone else carrying off the treasure. Even for preschoolers prizes may cause problems. Children over the age of 7 will probably be disappointed if there are no prizes for winners. If you do have prizes, be sure that everyone goes home with one.

- Consider nonmaterial prizes for young children if you elect to have competitive games: going first in the next game, sitting next to the birthday child at the table or the present-opening ceremony, or receiving a round of applause from the group. Have a team "chalk up" points so the whole team can be rewarded when the game ends.

- Use imagination to award prizes to nonwinners. They can be given for the best laugh, the hardest tries, the best sport, or even the brightest red dress; for the first to put hand on head or for being the best redhead at the party (assuming there is only one).

- Provide a grab bag of inexpensive prizes "because everyone played so well!"

- Self-stick badges and/or ribbons make flashy "winner prizes." You can pick them up in a teacher's supply store.

## Chapter 7

# What Games and Activities Can I Plan?

Unless you work with preschoolers on a regular basis, what will be newest for you is organizing and entertaining small children en masse. It's not tricky or hard, but it does take preplanning. Children left to their own devices usually don't come up with constructive fun activities—at least not ones whose creativity you'll appreciate.

Your game plan needs to be written out as well as thought out in advance (see Your Activity Planner, p. 76). It is important to tailor activities to your child's level of development. When in doubt about the appropriateness of an activity, you have your own test market. Try it out on your child! Do your "testing" well in advance of the party.

Above all, remember that young children like games and activities they are familiar with. Creativity on your part could actually be a drawback.

> *PICK GAMES YOUR CHILD LIKES AND*
> *IS GOOD AT. NOTHING IS HARDER ON*
> *A CHILD THAN TO HAVE TO PLAY*
> *SOMETHING AT HIS OR HER OWN*
> *BIRTHDAY PARTY THAT HE OR SHE*
> *CAN'T DO WELL OR AT ALL.*

# Which to Choose, What to Do?

Let your child have some say in this. Give choices or make suggestions instead of leaving the question open-ended.

Some games take too long to play, other don't take long enough. If you're dealing with toddlers, forget the games and read to them instead, or have a sing-along, or just let them play. At 3, children are ready for more structured activity, but include many of the easier games you'd use for a 2-year-old. Four-year-olds are open to a wider variety of activities.

- Play games that involve all the children and de-emphasize competition and prizes. Children can't handle defeat until they're about 7 (if ever!).

- Avoid elimination games. Otherwise, as children are eliminated you'll have to find something else to amuse them.

- Likewise, limit games that involve only one child at a time (pin the tail on the donkey, for example). When one child's turn is over, he or she often loses interest.

- Remember that races may bring out aggressiveness, and it may be hard to calm the children down afterward. However, if you have lots of running space (perhaps outdoors), races can be great for burning off energy. Relay races encourage team spirit and camaraderie.

- Don't get involved in messy things with more than a couple of children unless you're outdoors. In that case, finger painting or sandbox play can be fun for all involved.

- Remember that most inside games can also be played outdoors but that the reverse isn't always true. If you plan too many outdoors-only activities, what will happen to your party if it rains?

- Don't worry too much about games being too simple for older children. They like to "go back" and may be able to help teach younger children how to play.

## *Be Prepared!*

- Fill a box or basket with everything you'll need for each game or activity, and stack the boxes right in the game area.

- Keep an index card with all games and rules written down in the order in which they are to be played.

- Consider getting a whistle to wear around your neck. It brings the overly excited to instant attention.

- Plan activities that are both more simple and more difficult than you think the kids can handle. That way you'll be prepared if you've misjudged the kids' abilities or mood.

- Check with your library for books of suitable games, or talk with your child's nursery school teacher or a daycare worker for other favorite games the children all know how to play.

You can modify games to complement your theme or to go along with the season. Include such figures as clowns, hero figures, witches, reindeer, or bunnies, as appropriate.

One fun activity that also serves as a party remembrance is to tape-record interviews with the children. They delight in hearing themselves on tape. Avoid visible microphones, if possible, as they will be "eaten" or fought over. Questions to use for interviews can include, Why do we celebrate birthdays? How old are you? Describe what you look like? If your own child is overwhelmed by the day's events and prefers to tape his or her "interview" later, go with that.

*JUST AS THE BIRTHDAY CHILD IS
ENTITLED TO THE FIRST PIECE OF
CAKE, HE OR SHE IS ALSO THE FIRST
TO BE IT IN A GAME.*

- The order in which you do things is important. You should intersperse reasonably quiet activities with reasonably active ones to avoid chaos or boredom.

- If you have 10 or more guests, divide them into 2 groups for games. Let your helper play with one group while you help the others. Children aren't good at waiting and watching. This tactic will also prevent unoccupied children from wandering.

- Plan more games than you think you'll need in case some of them turn out to be too hard or don't appeal to the children. You may also be surprised at the speed with which some games can be played. One professional suggests planning at least twice as many games as you expect to have time for.

- Don't feel that you have to play all the games that you planned. Take your cues from the kids. If they are having fun with something, let them continue.

Don't force an unwilling child to play a game. The younger the guests, the more likely it is that some will not want to play every game. Have an alternative available, such as coloring or putting a puzzle together.

Activities and games have been grouped as follows:

- Arts and Crafts Activities

- Food-Related Activities

- Musical Games and Finger Plays

- Active Games (Competitive; Noncompetitive)

- Quiet Games (Competitive; Noncompetitive)

- Storytelling

# YOUR ACTIVITY PLANNER

**Craft Activities:**

_____

_____

_____

_____

**Time Estimate:**

_____

_____

_____

_____

**Craft Materials On Hand:**

_____

_____

_____

_____

_____

**To Buy:**

_____

_____

_____

_____

_____

**Games and Entertainment:**

_____

_____

_____

_____

**Time Estimate:**

_____

_____

_____

_____

**Other Activities and Materials:**

_____

_____

_____

**Time Estimate:**

_____

_____

_____

**Arrival Activity:** _____

_____

_____

**Party-ending Activity:** _____

_____

_____

**Other Items:**
Records _____
Games _____
Toys_____
Books _____
Songbook _____

## Arts and Crafts Activities

Crafts allow equal participation by all, without being competitive, and children are always proud and delighted to have something to "show-and-tell" about themselves, especially when the party is centered on another.

Having a craft project as an arrival activity instead of unorganized play can get your party off to a good start.

The craft activities listed here are appropriate for children 2 and up. They can be modified for different age levels. Pick what fits your interests, your party theme, or your child's preferences.

### T-Shirt Fun

Buy the most inexpensive plain white t-shirts you can find and let the children decorate them with crayons or permanent felt markers. Fabric crayons usually need to be heat-set, so send home directions with the shirt. If the kids are old enough and you have adequate help for supervision, give them a few iron-on patches for fancier shirts. Or let them make hand-print shirts by first pressing their palms in fabric paint and then pressing their palms on the t-shirt. Letter their names on their shirts with a marker.

### No-Mess Finger Painting

For each child, put ¼ cup of liquid laundry starch and 3 tablespoons of powdered tempera paint into a large resealable plastic bag. Squeeze out the air before locking the bag and seal it tightly with a piece of masking tape. Squeeze the bag gently to blend the paint and starch. The kids put the bags flat on a table and use fingers or hands to create pictures, "erasing" by smoothing out the bags. Try having them do it to music.

## Rock Painting

Let each child make a paperweight to take home, using small, smooth rocks and tempera paint. Mix some liquid starch with the paint to give it a consistency that adheres well to rocks. Be ready to help with suggestions—faces, flowers, animals—and encourage the kids to paint the backs as well as the fronts of their creations.

## Macaroni Necklace by Pattern

In a bowl, mix 2 or more kinds of noodles that can be strung. On cards, draw patterns of different arrangements of the noodles. Give each child a shoelace with a knot at one end and have him or her string the noodles following the pattern on the card. Younger children can work "free style." When the shoestrings are full, tie the ends together to form necklaces. Another variation for a stringing assortment is to use 1"–2" pieces of cutup straws in combination with large beads.

## Tin Can Planters

Collect an assortment of clean tuna, vegetable, and other small cans or styrofoam cups. Put a layer of pebbles in the bottom of each for drainage, then fill almost full of potting soil. Let the children plant small seedlings such as pansies or marigolds in the cans and pat down soil around them. Another variation of this idea is simply to let the children plant seeds that will sprout after they are home a few days. Marigold and bean seeds are two good choices.

Supply fine gravel or very small pebbles (or small seeds or yarn), white glue, and a small clay flowerpot for each child. Coat the outside of pots and one side of each pebble with glue, and when it's tacky, press the pebbles onto the pot in patterns or designs. (Cotton balls dipped in nail polish remover will help take glue off the children's fingers.) Let the pots dry thoroughly before filling or planting. Another variation is to use a plastic margarine tub or the bottom half of a milk carton for the pot.

## Vegetable Bin Folks

Put out an assortment of round and oval root vegetables, such as potatoes and rutabagas, and a quantity of buttons, fabric scraps, yarn, lace, sequins, cotton balls, and such. Let the children create bodies by stacking smaller vegetables on larger ones and connecting them with toothpicks. Dress the creatures by gluing on the scraps, trimming the clothes with the small items. Buttons are good for eyes, yarn for hair, cotton for beards.

## Bean Bags

Give each guest an old sock, a handful of dried beans or corn, and a sewing needle with a large eye, threaded with yarn knotted at one end. Set up a community workspace with scissors, glue, a stapler, felt-tip markers, and assorted scraps of fabric, felt, ribbon, and such. The kids cut off the toe end of the sock, fill it with the beans or corn and staple or sew it up tightly. They decorate their bean bags as they wish, then play a game of bean bag toss.

## Decorating Balloons

Supply plenty of blown-up balloons, tempera paint, brushes, glue, and any assortment of scraps of fabric, colored paper, feathers, glitter, and ribbon you can put together. The kids will do the rest.

### A Doll Like Me!

Cut child-sized lengths of paper from a big roll of brown wrapping paper or newsprint (your local newspaper may be able to supply this). Have each child lie down on one and quickly draw around the outside of each child's body. (Children over 5 can outline each other.) Let the children draw in facial features and clothing. If you wish, supply fabric scraps, buttons, sequins, and such for decoration.

### Easy Puppets

Cut the fingers from old gloves and have the children decorate the fingers, using marking pens, yarn, and scraps to make finger puppets. Or use old socks for hand puppets.

### Puppet-in-a-Cup

Give each child a cup cut from an egg carton, a regular paper cup, and a Popsicle stick. Let the kids use crayons to draw faces on the egg carton cups and give them scraps of yarn and cotton balls to glue on for hair. Poke holes in the tops of the heads and push the sticks through, taping the sticks securely on the insides. Poke holes in the bottoms of the paper cups and put the other ends of the sticks through them. When the kids push the sticks up and down, the puppets will pop up from the cups and then retreat back down into them.

### Play Dough

A batch of homemade play dough made up in advance can entertain guests at the beginning, middle, or end of the party. Supply resealable plastic bags so the children can take their creations home. Or give them a ball of dough to take home to play with. These recipes will make enough for 3 to 4 children.

## *No-Cook Play Dough*

1 cup white flour
½ cup salt
2 tablespoons oil

Mix ingredients and add colored water, a little at a time, until the mixture is the consistency of bread dough.

## *Stove-Top Play Dough*

1 cup flour
¼ cup salt
2 tablespoons cream of tartar (optional)
1 cup water
1 tablespoon oil
½ teaspoon food coloring

Mix flour, salt, and cream of tartar (optional). Combine water, oil, and food coloring and add to flour mixture.

## *Sewing Cards*

Use plastic lids from cans. Make holes ahead of time with a hole puncher, either around the edge or to form a design. Provide needles and yarn or shoelaces for decorating the lids.

## *Light Switch Art*

Buy plastic light switch plates to be decorated with stickers and/or permanent markers. Each child can design one to use in his or her own bedroom.

# Food-Related Activities

Not only are food crafts fun to make and "show-and-tell," they can also be eaten!

## Food Sculpture

Use any of the following for "handles": pretzel sticks, toothpicks, Popsicle sticks, wooden or plastic ice cream spoons, straws, or pipe cleaners. And any of these to stick on the handles in any desired arrangement: chunks of pineapple, apples, pears, or any other fruit; berries, grapes; mini-marshmallows or gumdrops; raisins or other dried fruits; pitted or stuffed olives; cherry tomatoes or chunks of other vegetables; cheese cubes; or chunks of lunch meat.

## Edible Play Dough

You can make a batch of dough (with or without your child's help) before the party and have it ready for the guests to play with and then eat during the party.

### Edible Play Dough

2 cups flour
4 cups oatmeal
1 cup water
1 cup white corn syrup
1 cup peanut butter
1 ¼ cups nonfat powdered milk
1 ¼ cups sifted confectioners' sugar

Combine flour and oatmeal in a blender and "grind" together for 30 seconds. Add 1 cup water and knead. Add corn syrup, peanut butter, nonfat powdered milk, and confectioners' sugar. Combine and knead well. Add more flour and/or powdered milk if the dough is too sticky to knead. Put out bowls of chocolate, butterscotch, or carob chips, sunflower seeds, and shelled peanuts for the kids to decorate their creations with and to make them tastier.

Variation: Mix 1 16-oz. jar peanut butter with 6 tablespoons honey. Add nonfat dry milk and/or flour until the peanut butter loses its stickiness. Carob or chocolate can be added.

## Edible Jewelry

Give the children blunt needles threaded with string and provide bowls of anything stringable: mini-marshmallows, Cheerios, licorice, raisins, olives, dried fruits, popcorn. Steam any hard vegetables first so the needles will go through them. Or use a string of licorice for stringing Cheerios and/or Lifesavers©.

## Bobbing for Doughnuts

Hang doughnuts from the ceiling with string and let the kids "bob" for them using their mouths but not their hands (but allow for some cheating!).

## Bread Dough Pretzels

Divide 1 loaf of thawed, kneaded frozen bread among 6 to 8 children. Let them roll it with their hands into long, narrow ropes and twist them into pretzel shapes or any other shape. Brush with beaten egg (optional). Bake at 325° for 15 minutes. Creations can be eaten and/or taken home.

## Peanut People

Supply a big bag of peanuts in the shell and a couple of packages of pipe cleaners. The children can create whole families of peanut people or a zoo of peanut animals by twisting the pipe cleaners around the peanuts for arms, legs, horns, or hats. They can paint on faces, too, with paint or markers.

## Food-Filler Spree

Fill a large container with trail mix, a cereal treat, or some other small-sized food. Let the kids use spoons to fill their loot bags with as much as they can for 15 seconds, or to the count of 10. Or allow 1, 2, or 4 "handful" grabs from a treat sack.

And see Chapter 5 for suggestions about decorative cakes, cupcakes, or cookies.

## Musical Games and Finger Plays

We all remember childhood songs a little differently, just as we all learned slightly different versions of familiar childhood games. Each song listed is one of the accepted versions, but feel free to use the words you grew up singing. The kids certainly won't know or care—in fact, if you listen closely, you may hear them singing a garbled version anyway!

- Teach little children songs by seating them on the floor in a semicircle and sitting in front of them on a low chair or stool. Keep a copy of the song (or songbook) beside you, in case you forget the words. Don't worry about your lack of singing talent; they're not critical listeners.

- Look also for special movement and games records and tapes, such as the Wee Sing series by Pam Beal and Susan Nipp, or mine on page 89.

- Remember, as you demonstrate finger plays, the children will mirror your actions and use their right hands as you use your left, and vice versa.

- Ask the children if they know any songs or finger plays, and let them teach you.

- Be sure that at least some of your songs involve action as well as singing. They'll offer something to do for children who can't sit still for long.

- Try having a parade with children's musical toys. Or a game of Follow the Leader, with the birthday child as the first leader. Be ready to step in and become the leader yourself if things get out of hand.

## Active Songs

### If You're Happy

*If you're happy and you know it,*
*clap your hands.*  (Clap, clap!)
*If you're happy and you know it,*
*clap your hands.*  (Clap, clap!)
*If you're happy and you know it*
*then your face will surely show it.*
*If you're happy and you know it,*
*clap your hands.*  (Clap, clap!)

(Subsequent verses can substitute for "clap your hands": "stamp your feet," "turn around," "swing your arms," "hug yourself," and "nod your head.")

### Ring Around the Rosie

(Children join hands and skip around in a circle, falling down at the end.)

*Ring around the rosie,*
*A pocket full of posies,*
*Ashes, ashes,*
*We all fall down!*

(Children hold hands and skip around in a circle during the chorus, stopping to act out the words of the song.)

*Here we go 'round the mulberry bush,*
*the mulberry bush,*
*the mulberry bush.*
*Here we go 'round the mulberry bush*
*so early in the morning.*

*This is the way we wash our clothes,*
*wash our clothes,*
*wash our clothes.*
*This is the way we wash our clothes*
*so early Monday morning.*

(Continue with "iron our clothes" for Tuesday, "scrub our floor" for Wednesday, "mend our clothes" for Thursday, "sweep our house" for Friday, "bake our bread" for Saturday, and "sleep in bed" for Sunday.)

### Head, Shoulders, Knees, and Toes

(Sing to the tune of "There Is a Tavern in the Town" and have children put their hands on each part of the body as it's mentioned.)

*Head, shoulders, knees, and toes,*
*Knees and toes;*
*Head, shoulders, knees, and toes,*
*Knees and toes and*
*Eyes and ears and mouth and nose,*
*Head, shoulders, knees, and toes,*
*Knees and toes.*

### I'm a Little Teapot

*I'm a little teapot,*
*short and stout.*
*This is my handle,*    (put hand on hip)
*this is my spout.*    (bend other arm up)
*When I get all steamed up,*
*then I shout,*
*"Tip me over*    (bend to the side)
*and pour me out!"*

### The Farmer in the Dell

*The farmer in the dell,*
*The farmer in the dell,*
*Heigh ho the derry-o,*
*The farmer in the dell.*
*The farmer takes a wife,*
*The farmer takes a wife,*
*Heigh ho the derry-o,*
*The farmer takes a wife.*

*The wife takes a child . . .*
*The child takes a nurse . . .*
*The nurse takes a dog . . .*
*The dog takes a cat . . .*
*The cat takes a mouse . . .*
*The mouse takes the cheese . . .*
*The farmer leaves the dell . . . etc.*
*The cheese stands alone . . .*

(Play with a minimum of 10 kids who are in a circle around the "Farmer." Children are pulled into the center of the circle 1 by 1 and then go back to their places 1 by 1, leaving the cheese alone in the center. The children clap along to the last verse, which ends the game.)

### Inky Dinky Spider

*Inky Dinky Spider*
*Went up the water spout.*
    (wiggle fingers to look like a spider)
*Down came the rain*
*And washed the spider out.*
    (hold hands high and bring down
    like falling rain)
*Out came the sun*
*And dried up all the rain*
    (extend hands over head in a circle)
*and Inky Dinky Spider*
*Crawled up the spout again.*
    (wiggle fingers to look like a spider)

### I Have Two

(Children point to each part of the body as it's named.)

*I have two little eyes*
*That open and close.*
*I have two little ears*
*And one little nose.*
*I have two soft cheeks,*
*And one little chin.*
*I have two lips that*
*close my teeth in.*

(Children use hands to act out mouse up, mouse down, and a single finger to indicate the clock striking.)

> *Hickory dickory dock*
> *The mouse ran up the clock*
> *The clock struck one*
> *The mouse ran down*
> *Hickory dickory dock*

---

# Party Music Sources

Two companies that offer records, tapes, and songbooks by catalog are:

Children's Book/Music Ctr.   Kimbo
PO Box 1130                  PO Box 477
Santa Monica, CA  90404   Long Branch, NJ 07740
1-800-443-1856              1-800-621-2187

Or just send for this Birthday Party music tape:

**Sing-Along Birthday Fun**
Book with music and art to color plus cassette of party favorites including "Happy Birthday To You" beginning both sides of the cassette so you can always find it in time when bringing in the cake!
$5.95 plus $2 postage.

By mail from: Practical Parenting, Dept BP2, Deephaven, MN 55391. Or call 1-800-255-3379.

## Active Games (Competitive)

When you're planning games for a birthday party, remember that kids love tradition. You may be thinking, "But they play that game at *every* party!" Your child will want it anyway because he or she knows the rules and likes the game. If it really is a game that's played at every birthday party, then his or her own party won't be complete without it.

### *Pin the (_____) on the (_____)*

Of course there's the "tail on the donkey," but you could just as well use the feather on the Indian, the backpack on the hiker, or the balloon on the clown's nose. Your imagination and your willingness to search out or draw big pictures are your only limitations. (Yes, you can buy a commercial Pin the Tail on the Donkey game.) Have more than one blindfold handy and at least one more adult to help you. The blindfold should not be so tight that the child can't see his or her feet. Don't turn a child around more than twice. The blindfold will be disorienting enough. Although some small children may be frightened of the blindfold (don't force them to play), this is an old standard, and most kids love it. For safety's sake, instead of thumbtacks or straight pins, attach small pieces of masking tape to the objects to be put on. Don't forget to put the child's name on his or her "tail."

### Duck, Duck, Goose or Drop the Handkerchief

"It" walks around the outside of a circle of seated children, tapping each on the head and saying "duck" to all but one, who's "goose." Goose gets up and chases It. When It is caught, he or she sits down and Goose becomes It. A variation is to have It drop a handkerchief or another small item behind the back of one child—more difficult to play because the children have to look behind them as It passes.

### Drop the Clothespin

Give each child 3 or 4 clothespins or other small items (tiny plastic toys, peanuts, pennies, wrapped candies). Have them take turns kneeling on a chair and dropping the items over the back, trying to get them into a hat or basket. The children can keep the items that go in. Or if you wish to have a winner, it's the child who gets the most in.

### Bean Bag Tosses

Your target for the bean bag toss can be as simple as a basket or hat or as complicated as the open mouth of a clown you've drawn and cut out from the side of a cardboard box. You can also hang a big bell from a tree branch and have the kids try to ring it by hitting it.

### Balloon Races

Have the kids hop to the finish line with balloons between their knees. Or give each child a different-colored balloon and have them walk, kicking their balloons ahead of them; or crawl on hands and knees, pushing the balloons ahead of them with their noses. Have plenty of replacement balloons on hand and be sure to dispose of broken pieces quickly.

### Balloon Break

Tie blown-up balloons to each child's ankles. The object is to break each other's balloons and to keep their own from breaking. The last to have an unbroken balloon is the winner. Best to play this one without shoes!

### Mother, May I?

The children line up, facing "Mother," who stands 10 or 15 feet away. Mother calls each child in turn by name and says, "You may take 1 giant step" (or 2 baby steps, or 3 hops, or anything Mother wishes). The child must answer, "Mother, may I?" and receive permission ("Yes, you may") before proceeding. Anyone who fails to ask goes back to the starting line. The child who reaches Mother first is the next Mother. In another version of the game, the children can try to sneak steps while Mother isn't looking, but if caught, they must return to the starting line.

### Simon Says

Have Simon face the line of standing children and give a command: "Simon says touch your toes." The whole group follows the instruction unless "Simon says" is left out, in which case they should not move. Anyone who does move is "out" and the game continues, with varying commands being given until only one child is left. Avoid the problem of what to do with those who are out by having anyone who makes an error go to one side or to the other end of the line and continue to play until one child reaches the head of the line. You might also substitute the birthday child's name for "Simon."

### Wheelbarrow Race

Divide the children into pairs. One child holds the legs of the other, who walks on his or her hands. When they reach the goal line, they switch positions and go back to the starting line. The pair that returns to the starting line first wins.

### Relay Races

Competitive and active, yet tempered by teamwork, relay races are for children over 4 and when you have 6 or more children at the party. You can race with an egg on a spoon; or hopping on one foot; or walking backward. One favorite is the clothes bag relay. Have 2 bags of similar clothes (a hat, a big shirt, old shoes, mittens). The child runs to a bag and puts *on* all the clothes. No need to tie or button! Then the child takes *off* all the clothes, puts them back in the bag, runs back to the team, and the next team member takes off to repeat the process. First team to finish wins.

### Velcro Toss

A target toss game using velcro balls is a good game for children. Young children can count how many balls hit and stick to the board; older children can keep track of their score.

### Shoe Mix-Up

Have all children remove shoes and place them in a pile, then mix them up. At a signal have everyone race for their shoes and put them on as fast as possible. This is best for 4-year-olds and up. You may wish to forgo tying of shoes as a criterion for "being on."

## Active Games (Noncompetitive)

### London Bridge Is Falling Down

Have the children stand in a circle, with 2 of them making an arch by facing each other with upraised arms. As music plays, the children walk through the arch. When the music stops, the 2 forming the arch drop their arms and try to "capture" the child going through. When 2 have been caught, they form another arch for the players to go through. When 2 more are caught, they form a third arch, and so on until only 1 player is left.

### Musical Chairs

This is a noncompetitive version of the old game in which the player who can't find a vacant chair when the music stops is out. (With the old version you end up with a lot of kids who have nothing to do while the game goes on.) Instead, play the music, take a chair away when it stops, but have the child who doesn't have a chair sit on the lap of one who does. Continue until all the children are on one chair, or on each other.

### Tag Games

Assign one "safety" position, such as squatting or holding the hands above the head, in which a player cannot be caught. If the game moves too slowly, limit the "safe" position to 5 seconds. Or have any person caught join hands with It and help catch the others until all are joined. Or play "Everybody's It," where everyone runs around tagging each other. Anyone tagged must stand still, with hands on head, until everyone has been tagged.

### Musical Laps

Have the children stand in a circle, each with hands on the hips of the one ahead. While music plays, the children walk around the circle; when it stops, each sits back in the lap of the one behind, but continues to hold the hips of the one ahead. It ends in giggles; everybody wins. (This might be best played without shoes.)

### Popping for Prizes

Slip small papers with numbers on them—one for each child at the party—into balloons, then blow up the balloons. Have the kids sit on the balloons to break them and get the papers out. The numbers determine their prizes. Carry the game a step further: have one child leave the room and let the others hide his or her prize. When the child returns, the kids can give clues by saying, "You're warm," "You're cold," "You're hot," or by humming, loudly for "hot" and softly for "cold." Best to keep a pin on hand to pop the balloon for any child who doesn't want to sit on it.

### Spin the Bottle

Have the children sit in a circle. Place a rolled-up message (words or pictures) in the bottle, spin it, and the person it points to when it stops takes out the message and does what it says. Message ideas: hug someone, rub your tummy, hop on one foot, shake hands with everyone, make the sound of the animal pictured, etc.

### Do as I Do Dance

With brisk music playing and the children standing in a circle, have one start the dance with a single gesture—raising one arm, perhaps. All the children do the same. The next child adds another motion, such as stamping a foot. Everyone repeats both gestures, and the dance continues, with each child adding something and then everyone repeating all of the gestures.

### Body Parts

Have the children stand around you in a circle. (You can supply a carpet square for each one to stand on, and send it home as a favor.) When you touch a part of your body (without speaking), the children do the same. Or call out a part of the body as you touch it, and the children do the same. Or touch one part of the body with another (toe to toe, arm to leg, ear to shoulder, toe to nose, wrist to lips).

Variation: Give each child a balloon to touch body parts with and to move under, over, between legs, in front, behind, etc.

### African Safari

Build a maze or obstacle course for "animals" to traverse. Each child can be an animal of his or her choosing. Use large boxes—singly or connected—for tunnels; a board can be a precarious bridge over a river; stuffed animals to jump over can be dangerous jungle animals to avoid. Once through the maze, the children are rewarded with an animal cracker.

## Quiet Games (Competitive)

### Memory

Set out an assortment of common, small household items on a tray, using just a few for young children, more for older ones. Let the children look at the tray for a few minutes, then take it away. Older children can write down the names of items they remember, younger ones can tell you, or you can make the game last longer by having them draw pictures. The one who remembers the most wins. Memory can also be played as a team game.

Variation: Put the items in a bag and have the kids feel them rather than see them, and then try to remember what they felt.

### Guess What I Am

The child who is It takes a picture of an animal out of a bowl or basket and imitates the animal until someone guesses what it is. The first child to guess correctly is It next, and the game can continue until everyone has had a turn.

### Guess the Sound

Tape some common sounds before the party. Then play the tape at the party and ask the children to guess what they're hearing. Tape the car starting, the toilet flushing, a clock ticking, a washing machine running.

### Beginners' Bingo

Make up grid cards like tic-tac-toe from heavy cardboard and print numbers from 1 to 6 in random order. You will need a die and pennies or buttons for markers. The first player throws the die and counts the dots. He or she then covers that number with a marker. Each player takes a turn and does the same. The winner is the first player to cover a row horizontally, vertically, or diagonally. Or it can be played until one player covers the whole card.

## L'Egg Hunt

Have a basket of empty L'Eggs™ containers placed in the center of a circle of children. One contains a small piece of ribbon. Each child chooses an "egg" from the basket and opens it. The child who gets the egg with the ribbon wins a prize. This can be turned into a noncompetitive game by having a small piece of ribbon in each container in one of any 3 or 4 colors. A blue ribbon, for instance, can let a child reach into a blue prize grab bag, etc.

## Unwrap the Package

With older children, play "Unwrap the Package." Wrap a small favor in several layers of different wrapping paper. The children sit in a circle and pass the package around as music plays. When the music stops, the child holding the package unwraps one layer. The child who removes the last layer gets to keep the favor.

# Quiet Games (Noncompetitive)

Though the classic game for small children is simply having them take turns dropping a clothespin in a bottle, there are other games you can try.

## Guess the Leader

The children sit in a circle on the floor, and It leaves the room while those in the circle select a leader who will start and change simple motions (pulling an ear, rubbing an eyebrow, twisting a lock of hair). The others follow the leader's actions, and It tries to guess who the leader is. Have It and the leader change places after 3 guesses. The game can continue until everyone has had a turn at being both It and the leader.

### Tell Me If I'm Wrong

Have an adult start the game by selecting a category of things children are familiar with: food, animals, furniture, etc. Speak fairly slowly and list a number of items, then throw in one that doesn't fit ("banana" in a list of animals, for example). The children call out *No*, raise their hands, or shake their heads when a word that doesn't fit is called out. Have children volunteer to be the caller, but be available for a little help.

### Fishing for Favors

Before the party, cut simple fish shapes, about 3 inches long, from heavy paper and attach a paper clip to each. Write numbers on the fish, 1 for each child who will be at the party. Make fishing poles from sticks and string and attach a magnet to the end of each string. The children "fish" until each one catches a fish. The number determines the prize. Everybody wins.

### Doggie, Doggie, Where's Your Bone?

One child is It and sits in the middle of a circle of children. It closes his or her eyes, and 1 child is given the "bone" (any small item will do). All the children sit with their hands behind their back, and It has 3 chances to guess who has the bone. If the child who is It guesses who has the bone, that child with the bone then becomes It.

### Cotton Ball

Blindfold 1 person and give him or her a cup and spoon. Spread newspaper on the floor and put 12 to 15 cotton balls all around. The blindfolded player tries to scoop up the cotton balls with the spoon. It's fun to do and watch!

### *Musical Magic Sack*

A grab bag with small, wrapped favors is passed from child to child in a circle while music (tape, radio, or piano) plays. When the music stops, the child who has the sack reaches inside the bag for a prize. Continue to play until all favors are gone. Or everyone can be a winner if you have the children move out of the circle as they win a prize. You may want to have them all wait until the game ends before they can open the prizes.

## Storytelling

Whether you can tell creative stories on your own or you are more comfortable sharing the written word, children delight in sitting around and hearing a story. This works well at any age. But it will not occupy a group as long as it does a single child (there will be too many distractions), so don't plan on more than 5 to 10 minutes of this activity.

- Read favorite stories, especially ones with action.

- Read storybooks with big pictures to show.

- Read with expression and drama. You may even want to have some props to accompany your tale.

# Winding Down the Party

### Pandora's Box: Opening the Gifts

Selecting the best time to open the presents can be tricky. The children, of course, will want to do this first, but most of us wait until the end for various reasons.

Some parents give their own gift to their child before or after the party. Others make it part of the party. For what it is worth, do remember that little kids are more often impressed by the size and number of gifts than by their value. To a small child, really good things *don't* come in small packages.

- As each child arrives, showing the gifts to those who are present and keeping things very low-key, downplaying the gift-giving and stressing friendship and fun. This may be a good practice for toddlers, who are often jealous and want to keep the gifts they bring. Show the gift to those present, then put it away.

- At the beginning of the party, after all the guests have arrived. It's wise to put the gifts away immediately so they won't get broken or have pieces lost before the party's over.

- At the end of the party, just before the guests go home. The advantage to this timing is that the gifts will be intact when the guests leave and letdown may be eliminated. It also lends a bit of mystery and suspense to the day's events.

## Gift Opening as an Activity

- Have the guests sit in a semicircle around the birthday child (and a parent, who will help as required), as nearly equidistant from him or her as possible.

- Consider letting the first present opened be a large plastic garbage bag filled with blown-up balloons. It makes a festive beginning and gives the guests something to play with while the gifts are being opened.

- Supply a receptacle for ribbons and wrappings and see to it yourself that these articles—and only these—get into it right away.

- Place the gifts in a stack by the child and encourage him or her to open them in order instead of rummaging through them for the largest, the brightest, or the best friend's gift. (Good luck!)

- Or let each guest hold one present and spin a bottle to select the order in which presents will be opened.

- Read aloud the card and the name of the giver and say something nice about the gift. Hold it up so everyone can see it (for the under-6 set, passing it around is unwise because the guests will be tempted to play with it).

- Or let each child hold the present he or she brought and give it to the birthday child to open.

---

## The Joy of Receiving

My 3-year-old's best gift was lunch bags with her name on them. One of the bags was filled with small sample packages of food, toothpaste, dried fruit, popcorn, etc.

*Jeannine Imhoff, Cincinnati, OH*

The best and worst gift my 3-year-old received was a flashlight. He refused to open any more presents after he opened that one.

*Alice Hoffer, McLean, VA*

When my son was 4, a neighbor gave him a padlock and key for a present. After the party, he said the lock was his favorite gift. He never locked anything up with it; maybe it was enough to know that he *could* if he wanted to.

*Katie Keefer, Edina, MO*

Our son's best gift was a "Balloon-O-Gram," which was a bouquet of balloons delivered to the door. He was thrilled.

*Kris Taranec, Lake Havasu, AZ*

---

- The box-within-the-box-within-the box routine where many boxes have to be opened to reach the final present is fun for the slightly older set, say 6 and up.

- Make a note of the gift on each card, for later thank-yous. Or keep a list (or have a helper keep one) as the presents are opened.

- Open only gifts from the party guests, not those from the family or others who are not present.

## Piñatas

The traditional piñata is a fancy, highly decorative papier-mâché animal filled with candy and toys. It is the central theme of children's birthday parties throughout Latin America and is enjoyed in North America, too.

Traditionally the piñata is hung by a rope or a pulley from a branch or hook above the children's heads. When it is on a pulley, the adult can raise or lower it out of reach of the blindfolded child who swings at it with a stick. (Each child is usually given 3 tries to break it.) The advantage of the pulley is that the adult can orchestrate, to some degree, when the piñata is broken so that each child can have a turn "at bat."

Older children are blindfolded, started out in the direction of the piñata, and given 3 or more tries at it. For younger children, forget the blindfolds—they'll be afraid of them, and just hitting the piñata will be enough of a challenge for them. Be sure the piñata is hung securely—pulley, or not.

This activity needs to be closely supervised as children must be kept out of the way of the stick-wielding child. A potential problem occurs when the piñata is partially broken and the contents are dribbling out. Children will rush in to pick up the candy while one child is still swinging away!

For my son's third birthday, I bought a piñata from a party shop and filled it with goodies (sugarless gum and healthy snacks). We hung it outside and everyone took turns giving it a whack with a broom handle. The piñata was so hard to break that even I had trouble, but no one seemed to mind. It took up a lot of time, showed everyone how to take turns, and had a fun surprise at the end.

*Debbie Parnakian, Huntington Beach, CA*

I don't like the idea of piggy children groveling on the ground grabbing as much as they can. Several children are always too timid to join the ruckus and feel left out of the booty. I prefer to give a small, plastic bag to each child and tell the children, "one bag per child" to eliminate the aggressive struggle to see who can get the most.

*Mary McNamara, Deephaven, MN*

## Do-It-Yourself Piñatas

- Make one as simple or as ornate as you wish. The easiest is simply to put several grocery bags inside one another. Decorate or not, fill with candy and toys, and staple or tie securely at the top. Or use a colorful paper shopping bag.

- To make a traditional piñata, start with a thin paste of flour and water. Cut long strips of newspaper—lots of them. Blow up a large balloon, dip the strips one at a time into the paste, and press them onto the balloon. Overlap the strips, covering the balloon securely several times, leaving one end uncovered. Let it dry for 24 hours or more, then pop the balloon and remove it. Fill the piñata with toys and candy and seal the end with more newspaper strips dipped in the flour paste. Decorate your piñata as you wish, making a clown face, a cat face, a jack-o-lantern, whatever. Use tempera paint and any assortment of scraps of paper or cloth. Tie yarn or string around it.

## Hunt How-To's

Children really love hunts at parties. Even 2-year-olds can enjoy a very simple hunt. Individually wrapped candy, inexpensive favors, and pennies are good treasures. Just be sure that everyone comes back with *something* to avoid tears and hurt feelings. Keep a few extra items available in case you have a slow "hunter." As children get older you can also offer a treasure hunt with clues.

- Make your outdoor hunt easy on yourself by hiding peanuts (lots of them!) around the yard, remembering that eye level for children is mighty low. Or hide peanuts or pennies in a big, opened bale of hay, or in a sandbox, if you've warned parents to dress their kids in play clothes. Caution: Don't hide peanuts or other food outside the night before the party. Squirrels or other animals might win the hunt before it begins!

- Wrap pennies individually in tin foil. It makes them easier to spot and takes time for children to unwrap them.

- Consider a "picture treasure hunt" for a small party, or divide the guests up into small groups of three or four and have several hunts going on at the same time. Use pictures of familiar household items like a TV, a sofa, a refrigerator, a dining room table. Give each group of children 1 picture and hide 4 or 5 others. On or under the TV set, for example, they will find a picture of a refrigerator, to which they move for the next clue. When they find the hidden treasure, there will be identical prizes for everyone.

- Try a "cake hunt" just before it's time for the food. Have ready a large puzzle you've made by drawing a picture of a glorious birthday cake on construction paper (the birthday child might help with this) and cut it into large, obvious shapes. Hide all the pieces in easy-to-find places, and when the kids have found them all, they'll "make the cake" by putting the puzzle together. Then . . . to the food!

- Put picture or written clues in envelopes labeled with each guest's name. The birthday child finds his or hers first, with verbal clues from you, opens it, and leads the whole group to the next clue. Each child in turn is leader, and when the treasure is found, it's divided among all the guests. Or the cake can be the treasure, with one clue leading to another, just for the birthday child.

## End of Party

By the end of a party, many children (including the birthday child) may be overstimulated. It's a good idea to have one or more quiet, cooling-off activities to end the party as you wait for the children to be picked up—something the children can drop or continue easily, such as coloring. Keep departures as happy as possible.

For instance:

- A new selection of coloring books and crayons to use, dot-to-dot books, rub-on Presto Magix™ transfers.

- An open-ended craft activity such as stencil tracing or using stamp and ink pads.

- A sing-along.

- Watching TV, a rented VCR tape, or a previously taped *Sesame Street* or *Mister Rogers' Neighborhood* program.

- Playing with your child's other toys. (But check with your child first and put away any toys your child would *not* like others playing with.)

> *HAVE A BALLOON OR SOME CANDY*
> *READY FOR A YOUNGER OR OLDER*
> *SIBLING WHO COMES ALONG WITH A*
> *PARENT TO PICK UP A GUEST.*

## Party Letdown

- Be aware that while you probably feel relief and perhaps a bit of pride that you've pulled it all off without major problems, your child will probably feel let down when the party is over and everyone has gone home.

- Have in mind something for your child to do after the last guest has left. Put on a quiet record and look over the presents together or read a new book.

- Or talk about the party. Find out what he or she liked best and least. Make some notes for next year's party; you may think you'll never forget this day, but you will.

- This can be the time to give your child the additional present from parents or grandparents.

- Invite one guest to stay a little longer to play, but don't let the other guests know—just ask the parent to come for him or her a bit later. Or keep one parent and a guest after the party, and while the children play the adults can have a quiet cup of coffee and a piece of cake.

- Plan another party to relieve the letdown, even if it's only a birthday party the next day for all the teddy bears in the house.

## *Thank-Yous*

- Offer simple thank yous at the door as the guests leave. Try to remember the gift and make a nice remark about it.

- Let a child make thank-you phone calls or sign off (or draw) on thank-you notes that you write.

- Use a photo taken at the party as a thank-you postcard or note.

- Send adults, especially out-of-town relatives, a photo of the birthday child with the gift received.

- Encourage your child to thank the guests by phone the next day, but don't insist. An articulate 3-year-old may enjoy doing this, but other children, some much older, will really balk.

- Some parents enjoy writing notes in the voice of their child; certainly a nice thought, but only if that is the type of thing you like.

# For Family Only

## Chapter 9

If you have an additional family party, be sure it's on a different day from the one you choose for the children's party to save both yourself and your child from nervous exhaustion.

- Have the whole family get up early and gather quietly around the birthday child's bed. Then sing "Happy Birthday" and present him or her with a small gift to start the day.

- Decorate the birthday child's place at the table for breakfast. Use balloons, crepe paper, a special birthday plate or place mat, etc.

- Make up a poem, song, or skit in honor of the birthday child. Let each member of the family contribute to it and have a part in presenting it.

- Let a child who's old enough select the party menu. For a toddler, select it yourself—you know what he or she likes best. In some families, each child's birthday menu is always the same, year after year.

- Use a special tablecloth, perhaps a plain white one that everyone can autograph each year.

- Consider saving the big cake for the family party and serve cupcakes at the children's party, especially if it's a very young group.

- Set up family birthday traditions right from the beginning. Some favorites: planting a tree or shrub in the yard each year; going on a special outing as a family (to the zoo, a park, a movie); or burning a big candle, the same one every year, for the number of minutes that corresponds to the child's age.

- Tape-record each family member recalling one or two favorite times spent with the birthday child during the past year, then play it at the party and save it as a keepsake.

- Show home movies of family parties from previous years for after-dinner entertainment. Or bring out old photos and home movies of the birthday child to see how much he or she has grown and changed.

- Involve older siblings in the plans for a baby's or toddler's party. They will enjoy the celebration more than the birthday child does.

---

**We celebrated 4 family birthdays at once with a cookout at noon on a blisteringly *hot* day with 27 guests! Our son was overwhelmed and so was I! Too many gifts went unnoticed and unappreciated.**
                                        ***Jodi Junge, Bryn Athyn, PA***

---

## VIP Treatment for the Birthday Child

- Write a birthday message on your child's bathroom mirror with lipstick. (It comes off easily with soap and water.)

- Make a special birthday badge with ribbons, lace, sparkles, and a big number showing your child's age.

- Make a birthday cape to help your child feel regal. You can go all out and make a crown and scepter, too. Or use the cape to incorporate a superhero theme.

- Set the birthday child's place at table with a special place mat, dishes, and glassware. You might want to buy a set just for these occasions.

- Make this the day you make annual fingerprint art or a plaque from your child's handprint. Save them and you'll have graphic proof of your child's growth from year to year.

- Start a birthday book of memories and add to it each year. It will make a wonderful keepsake.

- Make a certificate congratulating your child for successfully completing another year of life. You can frame and hang it, and replace it the following year with a new one.

- Buy a gift that can be added to each year: a string of pearls, a charm bracelet. It can be the beginning of a lovely birthday tradition.

---

## Birthday Clubs

A number of retail chains run "clubs" that you can register for at any time during the year. Their computer sends you a coupon to use at birthday time. Two good ones are Baskin-Robbins (which sends a coupon for a free single-scoop cone) and Walden Books (which provides dollar-off coupons on books for children).

---

# What About the Rest of the Family on Party Days

The birthday child is the *star*; this is one day for letting your child indulge in narcissism—pure and simple. Still, as the organizer of the party, you must consider the rest of the family, too.

## Siblings

Parties can be a source of jealousy for kids who are not the center of attention. Watching a sibling in the limelight is not easy. Many children misbehave to get their share of attention. Some special attention can help avoid disaster.

- Buy a small gift for a sibling, say some, especially if a younger one, to avoid jealousy. Others say, *Don't*. Siblings must learn that this is the birthday child's day and that they will have their own day in due time.

- Get out the photos and memorabilia from an older sibling's party when he or she was the same age as the birthday child. Besides the possibilities of getting some ideas yourself, you'll be showing the older child that his or her day was celebrated as wholeheartedly as this one will be.

- Perhaps the older sibling may prefer to come as a guest, ringing the front doorbell, or even under an assumed name.

- Let an older sibling invite a guest, too, and put the 2 of them in charge of announcing games, teaching the children songs, or helping to serve the food.

- Make plans to keep a younger sibling occupied and tended. Get a sitter or ask Grandma to come and be in charge of him or her (if that's Grandma's style).

Do get your pets out of the way for the party. You may prevent a disaster involving either the pet, a child, or both.

- Send your dog or cat out for trimming, bathing, shots, whatever, or to the kennel for the day. Or let your pet visit an animal-loving neighbor.

- Or lock pets in the basement or laundry room, if they won't be miserable there and howl or bark.

- Put even fish, turtles, or hamsters in a room where they won't attract the attention of children too young to handle them safely.

## Special-Occasion Birthdays

If your child's birthday falls on Thanksgiving, New Year's Day, Halloween, Valentine's Day, or another holiday, it can be a help, not a hindrance, when party time comes around. Your party themes and decorations are set for you, if you choose to use them, and planning timely games and food is relatively easy.

But if the birthday falls on or near a gift-giving holiday such as Christmas or Chanukah, your child may feel short-changed in both attention and gifts. And if it falls on that once-in-four-years day, February 29, you'll have some explaining to do!

## *Birthdays On or Near a Gift-Giving Holiday*

- Set up the holiday decorations on the birthday, if it comes before the holiday. If it's after, take down the decorations the day before and redecorate (lavishly!) for the birthday.

- Plan party themes and activities *not* related to the holiday, to keep the birthday a separate celebration.

- Move the party up or back a week or more and keep it separate from the holiday.

- Plan a party at your child's preschool or school after the holiday recess to emphasize the festivity away from the holiday setting of the house.

- For a child past the age of 4, an out-of-house party can help separate the birthday from the holiday, but don't make it a given. Let there also be parties on the home front!

- Consider a special "Twelfth Day" party for a birthday late in December or early January. The theme that immediately comes to mind, of course, is based on the old favorite, "The Twelve Days of Christmas."

- Let your child be "King" or "Queen for the Day." It's a way to highlight your child's day that can be separate from whatever is going on in the house for the holiday.

- Be sure *not* to double up on presents: "This is for your birthday *and* Christmas" is disappointing, no matter how grand the gift is. Wrap birthday presents in birthday paper, *not* Christmas paper.

- Set money aside during the year so holiday and birthday bills won't overwhelm you.

- Plan a half-birthday celebration in the summer, perhaps with an outdoor picnic, with or without presents. This might be a great opportunity to use the "grab bag" idea—each child brings one present, each takes one home.

- Remember to say "Happy Birthday!" before you say "Merry Christmas," "Happy Valentine's Day," or whatever. It's surprisingly easy to forget!

## Minimizing Midsummer Birthday Blues

On the other end of the spectrum is the July-August birthday when everyone is away on vacation or in camp. There is no school class to which to bring cupcakes. The scarce party population also makes for a limited number of presents. Whether now or sometime in the future, consider shifting your child's "birthday" six months ahead.

- Ask friends and relatives to cooperate. Ask that cards and presents be saved for the half-birthday celebration.

- On the half birthday, make two cakes, and save half of the second cake in the freezer for the actual summer date. Mark that day, but not with a party or gifts.

## Leap Year Birthday

- Celebrate the birthday for 3 years on February 28 or any other day during the last week in the month.

- But go all out when February 29 rolls around, and have a very special party. This first occasion will be on the child's fourth birthday, by which time he or she will be old enough to really appreciate unusual entertainment or a full-meal party.

## *Parties for Two*

If you have twins, you'll almost surely be doubling them up for a common party—few parents can handle two separate parties within a day or 2 of each other. Sometimes there are other reasons for joint parties—cousins or good friends whose birthdays are on the same day or very close together. If it's a very busy season, sharing a party will make it easier to find a convenient date. It's also a wonderful idea for a new-in-town child who hasn't yet made friends. There can even be some savings on such things as decorations. There are some precautions to take, though, so that each child feels the specialness that's supposed to be part of one's very own day.

- Try to invite guests both children know, and who know each other, just as you would for a single party.

- Plan on *two cakes*. Very important!

- Seat the birthday children at opposite ends or on opposite sides of the table and bring the cakes in separately so the guests can sing "Happy Birthday" to each child individually and so each can blow out the candles in the limelight.

- Encourage guests to bring 2 presents for twins, not just 1 that they can share. This is a bit tricky, but with tact, you can pass the word to 1 or 2 parents and hope they'll spread it.

- Make one part of the party special for each child—perhaps a special game for one, a special activity for the other.

- Have separate gift-opening ceremonies so each child can be the center of attention.

# Party Themes

## Chapter 10

Party supply stores or catalogs will offer many items featuring the current media fads, but any of the following ideas can be used just as successfully.

## Backyard "Beach Party"

Summer or warm climate special. Adds a bit of extra fun to a backyard party and can be as simple or busy as the age of the children permits. Advise parents that children should bring towels and bathing suits (or wear them under their play clothes).

- Refreshments: Picnic-style. Ice cream cones prepared ahead or ice cream cups; snow cones. The dish can be a Frisbee® (lined with a paper plate) to take home later. Lay blankets on the ground for eating.

- Favors: Sandbox toys that the children can play with at the party, then take home (get them in different colors and/or mark them with the children's names); balls; plastic sunglasses.

- Activities: Sandbox or sand-pile play; splashing in wading pool; running through the sprinkler, or jumping over the stream of water from a hose; finger painting or other arts and crafts; water balloon toss; chalk drawings on sidewalk. Search for hidden seashells. Mark areas for games on the grass with flour; it will hose off easily later.

- Variation: Teddy bear picnic (everyone brings favorite teddy bear).

## Backyard Snow Party

You'll no doubt serve refreshments indoors, but extremely cold temperatures or a blizzard could interfere with outdoor play, so have alternate plans for indoor activities. Let the parents know that the children should wear warm, waterproof outer clothing.

- Decorations: Hanging paper snowflakes; styrofoam balls of different sizes to make a snowman centerpiece.

- Refreshments: Ice cream balls to resemble snow; hot cocoa with mini-marshmallows.

- Favors: Sandbox-type toys for snow play; inexpensive plastic sleds.

- Activities: Give kids spray bottles filled with water, colored with food coloring, and let them "paint" snow sculptures they make. Make one big snowman together. A good game is Pie (make a big circle by shuffling paths through the snow, then make more paths to divide it into quarters; the children play tag but must stay on the snow paths); sledding.

## Circus/Carnival Party

How elaborately you carry out this theme will depend on the ages of the children. Balloons (helium or otherwise) and clown hats may be enough to make 3-year-olds happy; older kids can handle more excitement.

- Invitations: Blow up a balloon, write party information on it, let the air out and mail it in an envelope. Or place an animal-shaped note in an animal cracker box.

- Decorations: Lots of balloons (some blown-up balloons can be fastened to sticks, which are then stuck in the ground to mark the path to front door or the drive); circus posters; a "big top" swag over the table made of crepe paper streamers. Decorate the cake with plastic circus animals or frosted animal crackers.

- Refreshments: Hot dogs or clown-face sandwiches (see p. 48); popcorn balls; clown ice cream cones (pointed sugar cone on top of scoop of ice cream becomes a hat, decorate with candies to make face); a slice of ice cream (vanilla/chocolate/strawberry striped variety) becomes a circus wagon when pretzel or cookie rounds are added for wheels and two animal crackers are placed in front to pull it.

- Favors: Clown hats, balloons formed into animal shapes, whistles, hula hoops, box of animal crackers, circus coloring books.

- Activities: For 5- and 6-year-olds, entertainment by a clown who may help you make up the children's faces; a peanut hunt outdoors; making clown hats; drawing clown faces on paper plates; circus parade with toy musical instruments or stuffed animals, perhaps to the accompaniment of a record of circus music.

## Sports Theme Party

If your child is interested in a particular sport (soccer, T-ball, baseball, etc.), you can hire a high school "coach" to organize a game. The decorations and favors would be appropriate for the sport. This is very popular with kids and requires less work for the parents!

- Refreshments: Cakes can be shaped and decorated as a football, a bat, a soccer ball, etc.

- Favors: Paper megaphones, pennants, miniature sports equipment.

## Dress-Up Party

Don't feel you have to limit this party to girls or avoid the theme for an all-boy party. Boys love to dress up, too. Consider asking parents to send along contributions to the dress-up box, including old costumes of any kind, if you don't have a big collection yourself; they can be taken home after the party, if the parents have taped in a name label to help you sort them out.

- Decorations: Centerpiece of stacked-up hats of all kinds to use in dress-up. A full-length mirror with small balloons attached.

- Refreshments: Serve beverages in plastic wine glasses, sandwiches cut into fancy shapes, "cocktail" weiners, "hors d'oeuvres" of cheese cubes, fruit, or pieces of meat with fancy frilled toothpicks stuck in them, and other fancy canapés.

- Favors: Instant photos of the children in their dress-up outfits, perfume samples, jewelry, small purses, plastic hard hats, bow ties, canes, children's makeup.

- Activities: Let the children make a movie while they're dressed up. Hat-making for a craft: glue sequins, lace, and fabric scraps to paper plates, or make and decorate folded newspaper hats; make jewelry; put on makeup and nail polish or draw on mustaches and heavy eyebrows and goatees; draw, decorate, and cut out paper bow ties, and have the children tape them on so they can wear them home.

# Doll's Tea Party

This is a much-loved, traditional party. Very small girls won't need a lot of trappings, but you can go to more elaborate arrangements for older ones. Sharing of dolls may be allowed, but you may find that each girl wants to keep her own treasure close to her side. Don't forget to remind parents to send a doll along!

- Decorations: Set a table for the dolls with miniature dishes and food; guests' table should be set in tearoom fashion with flowers and candles.

- Refreshments: All the kinds of things grown-ups like, served on doll dishes, if possible—tiny sandwiches cut in dainty shapes (peanut butter is fine), decorated petit fours, ice cream balls cut with a melon scoop. In teacups, serve very weak, sweetened tea, ginger ale, or apple juice.

- Favors: Dollhouse furniture, doll clothes, and accessories.

- Activities: Playing house with dolls, sewing doll clothes you've cut out.

- Variations: Stuffed animal or teddy bear party; dress them up with scarves, ribbons, etc.

## Cowboys/Cowgirls and Indians Party

The West and its traditions still have a lot of appeal for children.

- Decorations: Make homemade "pow-wow" drums; use bales of hay for seats (outside or in a garage). Set up a tent indoors or out for a pow-wow.

- Refreshments: Chili as an option on hot dogs that have been cooked on a stick over a grill; coffee tins or mugs for drink glasses. If you're a camping family, some of your camping gear (mess kit for dishes, camp coffee pot for a pitcher for the drinks) can add the feel of "roughing it."

- Favors: Bandanas, water pistols, feathers, headbands, small plastic figures of cowboys, horses, and Indians.

- Activities: Water guns to shoot out candle flames; Duck, Duck, Goose (see p. 91) played as a pow-wow; singing cowboy songs or using cowboy music in any musical games; making and decorating a headband—with feathers—from construction paper.

## Pirate Party

Little kids love the "wicked" swashbuckling atmosphere. Consider reading a favorite pirate story while they eat.

- Invitation: Deliver a treasure map in a bottle, with the invitation on the back.

- Decorations: Hang skull-and-crossbones flags or use them as place mats; use black crepe paper streamers and balloons, and lots of tin foil.

- Refreshments : Chicken legs, potato chips, a square or oblong two layer treasure chest cake, decorated with jewels of jelly beans and gold coin candies; a red drink of cranberry juice or cranberry and orange juice mixed; or a cake with a "treasure" of candy hidden in each piece.

- Favors: Black eye patches, fake mustaches and beards, bandanas, scarves, small mesh bags filled with gold coin candies or shiny pennies.

- Activities: Treasure hunt, using one map for all, with a treasure to share at the end, or individual maps with separate treasures; fish for gold coin candies, which have been sunk in a treasure chest (see p. 98 for Fishing for Favors game).

# Backwards Party

Preschoolers and kindergartners are old enough to enjoy the concept of turning everything around backwards. Invitations can be executed in mirror writing, and the children can be asked to come with some clothing on upside down, inside out, or backwards, entering by the back door and saying "good-bye" just to get things started off "wrong."

- Decorations: Balloons and streamers tied beneath tables and chairs; posters hung upside down. Lay the tablecloth on the floor under the table, and have the children sit on the floor around it.

- Refreshments: Serve a meal in backwards order, which means the cake first! Give the children juice or soda in cans opened at the wrong ends, frost the cake on the bottom, use candles that relight when they're blown out; serve inside-out sandwiches made with meat or cheese slices on the outside, bread between them.

- Favors: Left-handed articles. Wrap favors with paper turned inside out.

- Activities: Give prizes first, being sure that each child gets one, then play any noncompetitive games backwards. Have a backwards walking race, or a bean bag toss, with the children throwing bean bags over their shoulders. Winners are losers, and vice versa.

# Color Party

Use your child's favorite color as the theme. For example, have red invitations, decorations, icing, and drinks. Have the birthday child and all the guests dress in red, and ask them to bring a red present (wrapped in red paper, of course).

# Artist's Party

Children are naturally creative. What better way to let their imaginations soar than with an artist's party?

- Invitations: Most museums have inexpensive artistic post-cards that work well as invitations. Or, fold a piece of paper to fit your envelopes, put a splotch of paint on the front and below it write "Artist's Party." Write the rest of the information on the inside.

- Decorations: Decorate the room with primary colored streamers. On the door to the party room, put up a sign that says, "Art Gallery" or "Artist's Loft."

- Refreshments: Cut the cake into the shape of an artists' palate. Or have the children decorate the cake (see page 45).

- Favors: Besides taking home the things they make, you can also include sets of markers, paint brushes or small paint sets.

- Activities: For an arrival activity have the kids work on a giant mural. Ask each guest to bring along a plain white T-shirt to decorate (see page 77). Buy inexpensive paper and let the children make stationary by providing stickers, glitter, gift boxes and ribbon to tie it together. Have the children build sculptures with anything you have on hand--pieces of wood, cardboard, beads, old jewelry, glitter, cork, buttons, ribbons. Be sure to have lots of glue, scissors and markers on hand. Or simply make sculptures with Play Dough. Try no-mess finger painting by putting a few spoonfuls of liquid paint into a Ziplock® bag (make sure you zip it closed!), and have the children fingerpaint by creating designs with fingers against the plastic. Hang a sheet over a clothesline and have the kids paint it with spray bottles of food coloring or water colors. Play music and have the children paint a picture of the feeling of that music. Photo copy favorite cartoons for the children to color.

# Prehistoric Dinosaur Party

You don't have to go far these days to find dinosaur items and activities. They have been popular with young children for decades.

- Decorations: Draw dinosaurs on paper plates, cut them out and use a paper punch to make holes in the top and bottom. Thread a straw through the holes and you have a drinking straw decoration. Write a name on the dinosaurs and these decorations become place cards. Small, plastic dinosaurs make good cake or table decorations. For a table centerpiece, shape frozen bread dough into a dinosaur shape (be sure to clip the dough on top to make a spiny back), bake and decorate. Or use a stuffed dinosaur toy to which you add ribbons and attach a helium baloon.

- Refreshments: Dinosaur cookie cutters can be used on thin slices of cheese, or for sandwiches. Serve Dinosaur Teeth (candy corn), Prehistoric Punch (make sure it's only a name, not a description of the age of the drink), Brontosaurus Burgers and Dinosundaes.

- Favors: Children's Museum gift stores are usually a good source for prehistoric paraphernalia. Books or coloring books featuring dinosurs are always popular. Plastic or rubber dinosaurs are readily available.

- Activities: Have a Dinosaur Race (i.e. wheelbarrow race). Have a Dinosaur Hunt by hiding small plastic dinosaurs or cut-out paper dinosaur "bones" inside the house or out. Disappearing Dinosaurs is the name of a reverse Hide and Seek game where the person who is "it" is the one who hides—the rest of the children look for the one who hid. One by one the "dinosaurs" disappear. The last one to find the group is "it" next time. Pre-record a Flintstones show and play it on your VCR as a quiet activity before the children go home.

# Fairy Tale Party

Fairy tales CAN come true (or at least to life) at birthday parties! You might even hire a "Good Fairy" to help you run the activities.

- Invitation: Add confetti or glitter to the invitation envelope.

- Decorations: Scatter confetti in a path leading to the party room, telling the children they're "fairy footprints." Make a gumdrop tree by hanging small bags of gumdrops on tree branches using ornament hooks. To make an outdoor fairy garden, cut out cardboard toadstools, giant paper flowers and beanstalks which you attach to garden stakes to create the fairyland scene. Hang tinsel-tied balloons, gum drops, or twinkling Christmas lights.

- Refreshments: Cut sandwiches with cookie cutters shaped like hearts, stars, butterflies and flowers. Serve pink lemonade. Hide a jellybean in one of the Jack-in-the-Beanstalk cupcakes, whoever gets it in their cupcake gets a prize. Frost a sheet cake with a rainbow and on top place a "pot of gold" (a small, spray painted cup filled with foil covered chocolate coins).

- Favors: Give fairy dust (gold and silver glitter). Make Magic Wands out of a large straw with a star taped on top and Christmas tinsel as ribbon. Make (or have the children make) as a take-home favor Tooth Fairy bags--anything from a little velvet drawstring bag to a lace trimmed pocket. Start each finished bag off with a little toothbrush or a quarter.

- Activities: Fish in a "pot of gold" for small prizes: use a large flowerpot spray painted gold or covered with gold tin foil and placed at the end of a rainbow made from cardboard. (Have someone be the helper and make sure each child hooks a prize). Choose your child's favorite fairy tale and either read it or have the children act it out--the birthday child gets the starring role, of course. Make construction paper crowns for each child. Have a hunt for Cinderella's Slipper by hiding a high heeled, single dress shoe. (Show the children it's mate so they know what to look for). Rent the ever popular "Cinderella" video. Read an abridged version of "Peter Pan" and make sure the children clap for Tinkerbell. Play musical chairs to "Twinkle, Twinkle Little Star."

## Rainbow Connection Party

There is nothing more upbeat or pretty than a rainbow theme.

• Invitations: Have the birthday child draw a rainbow on the invitation with magic markers.

• Decorations: Place a rainbow arch over the front door or hang rainbow streamers from the door frame for the guests to walk through. (If you've forgotten, the order of the colors of the rainbow is red, orange, yellow, green, blue, indigo, violet.) For background music, play the Muppets' "Rainbow Connection."

• Refreshments: Serve a multi-colored layered cake (see page 42). Easy to prepare and always impressive is rainbow layered Jell-O® in parfait glasses. Serve food on various colored plates, napkins and cups. Serve Neopolitan (tri-colored) ice cream.

• Favors: Look for inexpensive items featuring rainbows, from pencils to magnets to stickers. Glass prisms and kaleidoscopes are interesting favors if you can find them inexpensively.

• Activities: Draw rainbows on white helium balloons. Play "Color Bingo" or "Pin the Rainbow on the Pot of Gold." A treasure hunt activity's end will naturally be called the pot of gold. For an arrival or quiet activity, assign each guest a color, then have them look through magazines and cut out anything of that color to glue onto a sheet of paper. At the end of the party gather the sheets and tie them together to make a rainbow book for the birthday child.

# Space Theme Party

Space travel remains fascinating for children even though it has moved out of the realm of fantasy and into reality. Popular televison shows or movies (such as *Star Trek* or *Star Wars*) are easy themes to plan around.

- Decorations: White twinkling Christmas lights can give a starlight effect to a room or ceiling. Hang paper stars and moons or spray paint styrofoam balls to hang by a string for planets. Pull apart sections of fiberfill to form clouds to hang from the ceiling with white string or fishing line. Play the themes from *Star Wars, Star Trek* or *2001* as background music. For a place card, spray paint rocks silver, and write the guests' names on them. For a tablecloth, use slightly scrunched up aluminum foil. Tubes covered with aluminum foil make the basis of rocket ships

- Refreshments: Serve 'freeze-dried space food' like beef jerky, dried fruits, nuts and raisins, or real freeze dried food you can buy at any outdoors/wilderness store. Bake cupcakes and put tiny American flags in them. Use sparklers on the cake instead of candles.

- Favors: Activity or comic books with a space theme, Milky Way™ candy bars, small toy spaceships, balloons, space or space creature erasers, glow-in-the-dark stars.

- Activities: Play Hot Asteroid (hot potato), Astronaut's Bluff (like blindman's bluff only using spaceship sounds), or Moon Walk (hopscotch). Wrap a bag of peanuts individually in aluminum foil and hide them for a " moon rock" hunt. Have the children write about themselves on small cards, place them all in a tin can and bury it in the back yard as a time capsule. Get a large discarded refrigerator box and turn it into a space ship (be sure to include the control panel on the inside). Play the memory game "I'm going to the moon and I'm going to take a _____ with me." Each child adds an item to the list after repeating what has been previously said. To the tune of "Ten Little Indians" sing "One little, two little, three little astronauts..." Make "moon people" by drawing faces on half of a L'Eggs™ egg shaped container using clothespins for legs.

# Hawaiian Luau Party

What's more fun and festive than a Hawaiian Party?

- Decorations: Hang fish nets from the ceiling. Have big shells, strings of shells, real or fake flowers, and driftwood on tables or on the floor. Hang Polynesian travel posters. Use straw placemats on the table. Bring all your plants into one room to create a tropical look. Out of cardboard, create a cut out big palm tree and sun to put on the wall. Use an old trunk for a 'treasure chest' to place the gifts in. If it's winter, turn up the heat and encourage the guests to wear summer play clothes or even swim suits.

- Refreshments: Serve the commercial Hawaiian Punch or a home mixed version such as pineapple juice and ginger ale in plastic margarita glasses. Fruit can be served in a "dish" of a scooped-out pineapple, cantalope or watermelon.Make kabobs with cheese, lunch meats, fruit and pickles, then place in a bun. Or make a kabob out of fruit alone, served with a yogurt dip.

- Favors: Make candy leis by tying pieces of wrapped candy together with ribbons. Straw hats can be birthday hats. A real flower or small cactus plant can be a take-home gift. Shells can hold small candies or nuts and raisins can be covered with plastic wrap as a table take-home favor.

- Activities: Make grass skirts out of crepe paper strips or by wrapping a green sheet of crepe around the waist. Make green fringes by cutting up toward the waist. Play Don Ho music and do the hula or play musical chairs. Weave placemats out of paper strips. Make 'leis' by stringing LifeSavers® on string licorice. Make Kleenex® flowers. Sand play or art projects using sand will also fit the theme.

# Zoo Party

An exotic animal party appeals to boys and girls alike. It's something children are familiar with and lends itself to many variations.

- Decorations: Make cages for small stuffed animals out of shoe boxes by cutting out one side and using straws for cage bars. Decorate the cake with inexpensive plastic animals or animal crackers. Use crepe paper strips as "bars" to room entrances.

- Refreshments: What else but zoo animal fare? Put a sign saying "Seal Supper" on a dish of fish crackers, "Monkey Meal" on a plate of bananas, or "Elephant Eats" on a plate of peanuts. Animal crackers make good items to add to a snack cup.

- Favors: Wrap a small stuffed animal with crepe paper strips, forming a ball as you wind; tape small favors to the crepe paper at 7 inch intervals. Or try inexpensive plastic animals, balloon animals, or bags of peanuts. A box of animal crackers can be a take-home favor.

- Activities: Play animal charades by having the children act out animals that others have to guess; they can pull the name and picture of the animal to imitate from a hat. Let the children know that before they leave they have to give the birthday child a "Bear Hug." Of course, you could always have part or all of the party at the local zoo. Have an Elephant Hunt by hiding peanuts. Play "Polly Parrot" (Simon Says), using animal movements. (For example: "Polly Parrot says, swing your arms like an elephant trunk.") Have each child bring their favorite stuffed animal and have an animal parade. Check your video store for age-appropriate movies, ranging from *Dumbo* to *Born Free*. Read stories about animals as a quiet or ending party activity.

**Now it's time for you to get into action. Have a wonderful party!**

# Birthday Party Index

# BIRTHDAY PARTY MEMORY RECORD SHEET

Child_____ Birth date____/____/_____

Age (Circle one)    1    2    3    4    5    6    7    8

Day of the Week_____ 19 ___ Weather _____

Headlines of the Day:
_____
_____

Party Guests:
_____          _____
_____          _____
_____          _____

Food/Favors:
_____
_____

Games/Activities:
_____
_____
_____

Gifts Received:
_____          _____
_____          _____
_____          _____

# BIRTHDAY PARTY MEMORY RECORD SHEET

Child_____ Birth date____/____/____

Age (Circle one)     1     2     3     4     5     6     7     8

Day of the Week_____ 19 ___ Weather _____

Headlines of the Day:
_____
_____

Party Guests:
_____     _____
_____     _____
_____     _____

Food/Favors:
_____
_____

Games/Activities:
_____
_____
_____

Gifts Received:
_____     _____
_____     _____
_____     _____

## THE TAMING OF THE C.A.N.D.Y. MONSTER

Cookbook with healthful snacks, desserts, lunches, travel foods, milk-free cooking, micro quickies plus shopping tips. **$7.95**

## PRACTICAL PARENTING TIPS for FIRST FIVE YRS

Over 1000 best *"it worked for me"* ideas from diapering, toilet training, and childproofing, to getting kids ready for preschool, families on the go and sibling rivalry. **$6.95**

## FEED ME I'M YOURS

This bestselling babyfood, toddler cookbook has over 200 child-tested recipes, plus practical feeding advice for new parents.
spiral **$7.95**

## TOILET TRAINING

Advice on readiness, what to expect & how to motivate. Hints for daytime and nightime training. **$3.95**

## KOKO BEAR'S NEW POTTY

KoKo learns how nice dry diapers can be by learning to use first a potty seat and then the toilet. **$3.95**

## DEAR BABYSITTER HANDBOOK

Everything the sitter needs from vital numbers to a medical release form; play ideas, bedtime tips, & more. **$3.95**

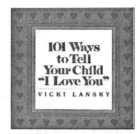